THE ANCIENT WORLD

10,000BC   **2500BC**   **1500BC**

▲ **10,000–3000BC** *Mesolithic hut,* EUROPE. A tent design made of wood, turf and branches.

▲ **c.2500BC** *Newgrange burial mound,* IRELAND. Great care was taken by the builders to ensure a dry resting place for the dead – unlike the flimsy domestic buildings the living had to inhabit at the time.

◄ **c.1304** *Abu Simbel,* ASWAN, EGYPT. The temple, built during the reign of Pharaoh Ramses II, was moved to its present site in the 1960s to avoid inundation by the Aswan High Dam.

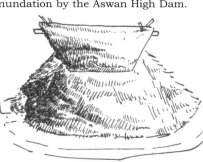

▲ **c.1000BC** *Jomon pit-post hut,* JAPAN

▲ **6000BC–present** *Idlib house,* IRAQ. Mud-covered (*adobe*) houses like these may have been the first permanent settlements of agrarian communities.

▲ **2778BC** *The Step-Pyramid of Zoser,* SAQQARA, EGYPT. The first building with a named architect – Imhotep.

▶ **c.1100BC** *Temple of Amun,* KARNAK, EGYPT. A temple complex which, together with Luxor, is all that remains of Thebes, the capital of Ancient Egypt.

▼ **2125BC** *The Great Ziggurat of Ur,* IRAQ. Temple to the moon-god Nar na, built of mud bricks.

▲ **3000BC–present** IRAQ. Marsh Arab (*Ma'dan*) reed-constructed mudhif or guest house.

▶ **2100BC** *Stonehenge,* WILTSHIRE, ENGLAND. Begun as early as 3000BC the 80 Pembroke blue stone pillars in two concentric circles are early third millennium.

▼ **2575BC** *The Great Pyramid of Cheops,* GIZA, EGYPT. Originally covering 13 acres (5.26 ha) the Great Pyramid (*center*) was twice the size of St Peter's, Rome.

▲ **c.550BC** *The Ishtar Gate,* BABYLON (*now in the National Museum, Berlin*). Glazed brickwork decorated with heraldic beasts, the Ishtar Gate stood at the head of King Nebuchadnezzar's Processional Way.

▼ **c.600BC** *Etruscan tumuli,* CERVETERI, ITALY. A burial chamber which originally formed part of a large necropolis serving the Etruscan city of Caere.

▶ **c.1600BC** *The Palace of Minos,* KNOSSOS, CRETE. Constructed of stone blocks, rubble filling and mud bricks. Wood columns taper towards the base – the opposite of later Greek buildings.

▲ **c.447BC** *The Parthenon,* ATHENS, GREECE. A temple dedicated to the goddess Athena, the Parthenon is the most beautiful example of the Doric Order, the simplest of the three Orders: Doric, Ionic, Corinthian.

10,000BC   **2500BC**   **1500BC**   **500BC**

c.10,000BC – THE BIRTH OF FARMING. The first evidence of cultivating plants for food is in Mesopotamia. Humans evolve from hunter-gatherers to farmers.

c.6500BC – RICE IS CULTIVATED IN CHINA. Farming communities develop along the Yellow and Yangtze rivers.

c.3500BC – THE INVENTION OF WRITING. Sumerians replace pictograms with cuneiform, a series of strokes made by a reed on a damp clay tablet. The sun-baked tablets are the earliest written records.

c.3150BC – EGYPT RISES. The civilization of ancient Egypt begins in the Nile Valley when Upper and Lower Egypt are united.

EGYPTIAN ROYAL MALE

c.1700BC – THE FIRST LEGAL SYSTEM. The Code of Hammurabi, King of Babylon, defines criminal laws, inheritance laws, and promises to treat conquered peoples justly.

1200–00BC – A SURE-FIRE BESTSELLER. The Old Testament or Bible is first written. Its language is Hebrew, with occasional passages in Aramaic.

ANCIENT GREEK

776BC – ULTIMATE SPORTS. The first Olympic Games are held by the Greeks in Olympia. The Games last for 7 days and include religious ceremonies.

750BC – CELTS AND SALT. The Celts, from the Hallstatt region of central Europe, cross the Alps to trade with the Greeks. They exchange salt for luxury goods, spreading their civilization in all directions.

563BC – FATHER OF BUDDHISM IS BORN. Buddhism springs from the teachings of Siddharta Guatama, who comes to be known as the Buddha or "enlightened one."

Architect biographies

SINAN
1489–1588

SINAN WAS BORN a Greek Christian in Anatolia, Turkey in 1489. In 1512, he was drafted into the Ottoman army, converted to Islam, and trained to fight for the Sultan. He was taught the trade of carpentry, and quickly advanced to the rank of construction officer, which had him building fortifications, ships, and bridges. His gifts led to his appointment as chief architect to Sultan Suleiman ("the Magnificent") in 1538. For the next 50 years, until his death at the age of at least 90, he designed and built 133 mosques, 55 schools, 34 palaces, 33 public baths, 22 mausoleums, 3 hospitals, 16 alms houses, 7 madrasas (Islamic schools), 8 bridges, and 12 caravansaries or commercial buildings.

Mosques were Sinan's crowning achievements, and three of them illustrate the three distinctive stages of his career. Sinan himself called the Shehzade Mosque (1542) an "apprenticeship" work; the Suleimaniye Mosque (1557) a "journeyman" work; and the Selimiye Mosque (1574) his "master" work. Shehzade uses four half domes to link the central dome with the rest of the complex. Suleimaniye moves in the same direction on a much larger scale. Modeled after the great Byzantine Hagia Sofia in Instanbul (6th century), it includes not only a central mosque, but also a medical college, two mausoleums, numerous baths, a hospital, and four madrasas. Although exquisite and monumental, it does not yet achieve its creator's aim of an absolute unified internal space. That comes with the Selimiye Mosque in Edirne, Turkey. Here, Sinan executed his perfect centralized plan with a towering dome supported by eight interior columns and buttresses, and minarets at each corner framing the entire structure. Dazzling color, decorative components, and the choice of site contribute to Selimiye's standing as a groundbreaking masterpiece of harmonious design.

Suleimaniye, Istanbul

While Sinan's contemporaries in Renaissance Italy were working their own magic with domed structures, none of them built on a scale remotely approaching his one hundred plus domed buildings. Sinan was the very face of Classical Ottoman architecture. His influence extended centuries beyond his death in 1588, and his works – testaments to the strength and sophistication of Ottoman culture – remain great emblems of Turkish pride.

SIR CHRISTOPHER WREN
1632–1723

WREN'S PATH TO ARCHITECTURE was not a predictable one. He was born in 1632 in East Knoyle, Wiltshire, the son of the rector. He was consumed with science and math as a boy, and by the time he entered Oxford at age 17, he had already invented an instrument that wrote in the dark, a pneumatic engine, and a new language for the deaf. He was made Professor of Astronomy at Gresham College, London at age 25, and Professor of Astronomy at Oxford at age 29.

Nepotism is what got Wren his first architectural commission. His uncle, the Bishop of Ely, got him the job of designing Pembroke College Chapel at Cambridge University (1663). He followed that with the Sheldonian Theatre in Oxford (1664–69), and started to make his reputation as an architect. The Great Fire of London (1666) was a watershed event in Wren's architectural career, as it prompted his master plan for the rebuilding of the city. His bold scheme of replacing London's narrow streets and snaking alleys with wide boulevards was not adopted. But Wren was appointed one of the architectural commissioners for the rebuilding project, with special responsibility for the rebuilding of London's churches.

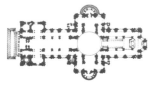

St Paul's, London

St. Paul's Cathedral in London (1675–1710) is Wren's undisputed masterpiece. The great dome towering over the church is an architectural and engineering wonder – grand, elegant, perfectly-formed, solid. Wren had to alter his original central Greek cross plan for the church when the clergy deemed it too Catholic. They insisted on a traditional medieval plan, cruciform-shaped, and Wren obliged – but not without eventually sneaking in elements from his original plan.

Wren's other notable London churches include St. Stephen's, Walbrook; St. Martin, Ludgate; St. Bride, Fleet Street; St. James, Piccadilly; and St. Mary Le Bow, Cheapside, among many others. St. Mary Le Bow was the first to boast Wren's great Classical steeple, which came to be an architectural fingerprint of sorts. His secular public works include the library of Trinity College, Cambridge; the library of Queens College, Oxford; the Royal Hospital, Chelsea; the Royal Hospital, Greenwich, and the garden façade of Hampton Court Palace. His contributions to English architecture were so enormous – and so admired – that he was knighted in 1675. He died at the age of 90 and was buried in his own masterpiece – St. Paul's Cathedral.

FRANK LLOYD WRIGHT
1867–1959

BEGINNING with only a brief period of study at the University of Wisconsin and apprenticeship with the famous Chicago architect Louis Sullivan, Wright set up his own practice in 1893. His work for the next 15 years was a model of success combined with principle as he developed the Prairie House, characterized by its spreading eaves, solid chimney mass, leaded-glass windows and specially designed furniture. This initial body of work was a stunning interpretation of traditional architectural elements.

Frustration with work and family led him to flee to Europe with a client's wife. On his return he built his home and studio, Taliesin (a name from his mother's Welsh heritage) in 1911 at Spring Green, Wisconsin. Taliesin shows a greater freedom from axial design and a deeper sympathy for the site – an exploration of freedom and order.

For the next 20 years he experimented with various materials and geometries as he worked in Japan and California. Wright returned to America in 1938 and built Taliesin West, a brilliant adaptation to its Arizona desert landscape.

In his 60s Wright took his spatial and structural principles to new heights with his Usonian houses, 'Fallingwater', the Johnson Wax headquarters, and the Guggenheim Museum, New York. A comparison of the Guggenheim (Wright's design dates from 1943) with the Unity Temple, Oak Park (1905) illustrates the similarities and disparities. Both are made of concrete, both have two masses with a central entry, both have balconies overlooking a central space lighted from above. Unity Temple, however, is rectilinear and assembled from blocks; the Guggenheim is circular with a thin ribbon serving as structure and volume at once. They represent "continuity" and "plasticity" – what he thought architecture should be.

From the classic symmetry of his first house, the Winslow house of 1893–4, to the incredible explosion of ornament in Midway Gardens of 1914, the Imperial Hotel, Japan of 1922–28, the drama of 'Fallingwater', to the planning proposal for Broadacre City, Frank Lloyd Wright's powerful imagination, his "honest arrogance", and his complete dedication to his art place him in the very highest rank of the architectural Pantheon. One can be moved or agitated by his work (as well as his personality) but he remains the most intriguing and masterful American architect whose range is unmatched.

Wright. Interior, Unity Temple

close to completion. He devoted 16 years of his life to its construction, taking up residence on the site and living there like a hermit. To say there is no more unconventional church in Europe is an understatement. What started as a Gothic structure gave way to a more free-flowing composition, and a test of new structural possibilities. The nativity façade, apse, and crypt (where Gaudi is buried) were the only portions completed in Gaudi's lifetime.

Gaudi died when he was run over by a street car on Barcelona's Gran Via. Initially, nobody recognized the old man, and he was taken to a public ward in a local hospital. When his identity was discovered, Barcelona gave him something akin to a state funeral. Efforts are underway by some Catholic clergy to go one better than that: they want to canonize him.

MIES VAN DER ROHE, LUDWIG
1886–1969

In 1953 some of Mies's students asked him why he had never written a book. Mies looked astonished. "Why should I write a book?" he said, "If people want to know what I have to say, they should look at my buildings."

BORN IN AACHEN, Germany, the son of a stonemason, Ludwig Mies van der Rohe attended the cathedral school and a technical high school, and that was as far as his formal education went.

Between 1919 and 1923 a series of five unbuilt projects, including two visionary, all-glass, skyscrapers firmly established Mies as one of the leaders of the rising Modern movement in German architecture.

By the end of 1928 he was at work on two projects destined for immortality: the German Pavilion at the International Exposition in Barcelona, and the Tugenhadt House in Brno, Czechoslovakia. The Barcelona Pavilion was constructed in the spring of 1929, dismantled at the end of the Exposition in 1930, fully rebuilt in 1986, and established itself as a pole-star of 20th century architecture. Space

Barcelona Pavilion

in the Pavilion is fluid, defined by vertical planes rather than enclosed by walls which, here, are mere abstractions. Interior and exterior seamlessly inter-react. Chromium-plated steel columns are seen against, and independent of, the space-defining planes, asserting the structural grid. The other materials used in the Barcelona Pavilion were Roman travertine, Tinian marble, onyx, and gray glass.

The same spatial approach and similarly rich palette of materials were used in the Tugendhat house, all adapted to serve the needs of family living and accommodation of the site. Some criticism has been made of Mies's so-called indifference to the site of his

buildings. Nothing could be further from the truth. From the beginning to the end of his career he adopted a system of photographic collaging to superimpose drawings or photographs of his intended building on photographs of the site. As a small but significant example illustrates, the giant maple tree that was on the site of the Farnsworth House (begun 1945) was included in all of Mies's plans and carefully incorporated into the final execution.

In 1930 Mies was invited to become the Director of the Bauhaus (the foremost modern design institution of its day, but then on the point of collapse after two years of disastrous leadership by Hannes Meyer). He took on the task and completely revitalized the Bauhaus which, however, could not escape the Nazi hatred of Modernism, and was forced to close in 1933.

Driven from Germany, Mies emigrated to America in 1938 and became head of the School of Architecture at the Illinois Institute of Technology, Chicago, where he put in place an entirely new curriculum and undertook the design of a new campus. Mies's ITT campus designs (begun 1940) were soon followed by the twin glass-and-steel towers at 860–880 Lake Shore Drive, Chicago, a building type that he was to re-study, repeat and refine until it culminated in the Seagram Building, New York, in 1956 (which a leading critic has hailed as "the building of the millennium.")

It was the pursuit of the essentially one-room, clear span building, such as the Farnsworth House (1945–49), Crown Hall (1952–54), the unbuilt Chicago Convention Hall and others, which led Mies to his final and crowning masterpiece, the New National Gallery, Berlin, completed in 1968.

Mies's buildings are meant to teach a lesson; reflecting with brilliant clarity the principles on which his architecture was founded. They may captivate us with their elegant proportions, impeccably crafted details or masterful adaptation to site, but their main goal was to contribute to the creation of a new language for architecture: an everyday language that could be spoken by everyone.

In the past, Western architecture had produced two vocabularies: the Gothic and the Classical. The Gothic used groined vaults, pointed arches and flying buttresses give a clear and forceful expression of structure with emphasis on each constituent element in the overall composition. The Classical had its Orders, domes, arcades, and plinths to convey the spirit of unity, serenity, and repose. The usefulness of these vocabularies ended with the eclecticism of the 19th century. The modern architecture that began to emerge at the beginning of the 20th century was chaotic in its variety, and it was this void that Mies sought to fill with logic, clarity, and order. The National Gallery, Berlin, Mies's last work, is a perfect example in which the structure is strongly and clearly revealed and forcefully articulated but which conveys a profound serenity and order.

Some critics have accused Mies of creating merely generalized buildings, "universal spaces", which did not express the nature of the building or the functions they were to house. Mies, however, realized that modern society – especially in the USA – was based on continuous change and that buildings would have to be designed to adapt to different functions. His genius was to create the possibility of change in a context of serene rationality.

ANDREA PALLADIO
1508–1580

"Guided by a natural inclination, I gave myself up in my most early years to the study of architecture." Palladio

PALLADIO was born Andrea di Pietro della Gondola in 1508 in Padua. At age 13, he left an apprenticeship with a Paduan stonecutter to flee to Vicenza, near Venice, where he honed his craft of stonemasonry. As a young man he went to Rome to study the ancient monuments and the leading theorists of the Renaissance, as well as Vitruvius.

Much of Palladio's architecture consists of country villas and urban palaces such as the Villa Barabaro, c.1554. The Villa Capra (Rotonda) (Vicenza, 1550–59) is one of the finest examples of his particular brand of classicism. It consists of a square block surmounted by a dome, with porches on each side in the shape of Roman temple pediments. While the classicist Alberti had described a plan like this as ideal for a church, it was highly unusual to use such a design for a house. The Villa Rotonda was significant as a new type of house: not a functional everyday house, but an elegant retreat for the wealthy to escape their daily lives.

Villa Capra, Vicenza

Commissions to design in Venice itself finally came to Palladio in the 1560s. His work there culminated in three splendid churches: San Giorgio Maggiore (1560–80), San Francesco della Vigna (1562–70) and Il Redentore (1576–91). At San Giorgio Maggiore, he faced head-on the problem of placing a Classical temple-front on a basilican church. His solution was novel: high, narrow temple-fronts are placed at the ends of the naves, with wider, lower temple-fronts set behind them, outlining the aisles. Inside, the church is a paean to the Renaissance ideals of clarity, proportion and light, with a gray and white color scheme reminiscent of Brunelleschi's Pazzi Chapel.

Palladio also favored Venice and environs with civic buildings such as the Teatro Olimpico (Vicenza, 1580) – the first permanent theater since antiquity. The Basilica Vicenza where he wrapped a perfect two-story classical loggia around the existing Gothic structure.

It was the publication in 1570 of The Four Books of Architecture that secured Palladio's place forever in architectural history. The writings articulated not only Palladio's philosophy of design, but also laid out practical advice for building.

Palladio has had many followers and Palladianism many revivals. Some of his most celebrated followers, great architects and thinkers in their own right, were Inigo Jones, in the early seventeenth century; Lord Burlington, in the early eighteenth century; and Thomas Jefferson in the mid-eighteenth century in America. Jefferson's Virginia residence, Monticello, is probably the most famous Palladian building in America, although Palladian style was popular almost from the country's birth. Palladian-influenced buildings can be found all across America and the world.

▲ **c.350BC** *The theatre of the Sanctuary of Asklepios*, EPIDAURUS, GREECE. Designed by Polykleitos the Younger.

▲ **c.200BC-present** *Yurt*, MONGOLIA. A tent-like structure made of willow poles covered in oiled felt. Today almost two-thirds of the population of Mongolia still live in yurts which are now factory-made.

◄ **c.AD14** *Pont du Gard*, NIMES, FRANCE. Roman aqueduct built by Agrippa, it was originally 15 miles (24km) long. Th water channel on the top level is 180ft (55m) above the river.

c.221BC *The Great Wall of China.* 2,484 miles (825km) of fortification, the present Wall belongs mainly to the Ming Dynasty (AD14–16 centuries).

▼ **c.200BC** *The Great Stupa*, SANCHI, MADYA PRADESH, INDIA. Originally a small unimposing burial mound (*stupa*), the Great Stupa grew in size as Indian Buddhism became wealthier.

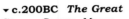

◄ **AD70** *The Colosseum* ROME, ITALY. Designed to seat 50,000 people the vast elliptical amphitheatre measures 615ft (188m) by 510ft (156m).

▼ **118–133** *Hadrian Villa*, TIVOLI, ITALY. Th Emperor Hadrian fille his palatial country retreat with a vas collection of statuary an artworks from Ancien Egypt an Classica Greece

► **c.118–128** *The Pantheon*, ROME, ITALY. The most important temple of its day, the dome (142ft/43.2m in diameter) was the largest until Brunelleschi's dome for Florence Cathedral (1420–36).

► **c.120** *The Treasury*, PETRA, JORDAN. Petra (from the Greek word for 'rock') was the capital of the Nabuteans who controlled the caravan routes between Arabia and the Mediterranean.

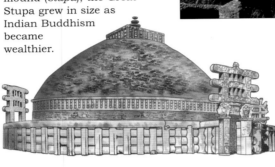

▲ **c.200BC** *House of the Vetii*, POMPEI, ITALY. An elegant Doric colonnade surrounds the garden of a wealthy Pompeian family.

◄ **c.100BC–present** *Samoan fale tele* (great house). The largest ever recorded had a diameter of 53 feet (18m).

► **c.200–present** *Ruma gorga* decorated house of the Toba Batak people of Lake Toba, SUMATERA, INDONESIA.

▲ **c.200BC** *Celtic stone and thatch hut,* GALICIA, SPAIN

▲ **c.AD1** *Maison Carrée*, NIMES, FRANCE. One of the best-preserved Roman temples, it was probably built by craftsmen sent to Nemausus (ancient Nimes) from Rome.

347BC – PLATO DIES. The great Greek scholar's influence on western philosophy lives on to the present day.

339BC – ALEXANDER THE GREAT CONQUERS PERSIA. Alexander III, king of Macedon, spreads Greek culture far and wide in a journey of conquest lasting 11 years and spanning 20,000 miles.

300BC – JAPAN EMERGES. Rice farms appear in Japan, presaging the unified kingdom of Japan that will develop over the next 600 years.

264BC – ROMAN SHOWMANSHIP. The first public performances of gladiators, specially trained to fight each other to the death, are held in amphitheaters.

149BC – CHINESE WORD WEALTH. An ancient Chinese dictionary contains 10,000 characters.

110BC – THE SILK ROAD OPENS. Trade between Han China and western Asia and Europe flourishes along this route.

100BC – JULIUS CAESAR BORN. Caesar is the first Roman emperor to be worshiped as a god. He rules the Roman Empire until he is assassinated in 44BC.

ROMAN SOLDIER

46BC – A YEAR IN THE LIFE. The Julian calendar of 365.25 days is adopted. Leap year is introduced.

6BC–AD30 – LIFE OF JESUS CHRIST. The historical evidence points to this period as the probable life span of the religious leader.

AD250 – MAYAN CIVILIZATION FLOURISHES. The Native Americ people of Central America bu a sophisticated culture that is its peak from 250–900AD.

330 – AN EMPIRE DIVIDED. The Roman Empire is spl into two: Western, run fr Rome; Eastern (Byzantine from Constantinople.

FIRST MILLENNIUM AD

432–440 Interior of S. Maria Maggiore, ROME, ITALY. An early example of a basilica-type church (rectangular rather than round or octagonal like S. Vitale, Ravenna – see 526).

523 The Pagoda of the Sung Yüeh Temple, MOUNT SUNG, HONAN, CHINA. The oldest surviving brick temple in China.

c.550 Rock-cut temple, ELEPHANTA, MAHARASHTA, INDIA. Hindu temple dedicated to Shiva Natarja, the god of creation and destruction.

569 Temple of the Magician, UXMAL, MEXICO.

680 Brixworth Church, ENGLAND. A rare example of a wood-roofed Saxon church.

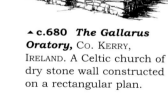

c.680 The Gallarus Oratory, CO. KERRY, IRELAND. A Celtic church of dry stone wall constructed on a rectangular plan.

526–48 S. Vitale, RAVENNA, ITALY. The best preserved Byzantine church in the west. It was founded by Emperor Justinian.

c.690 Temple of the Sun, PELENQUE, MEXICO. The decorative roof-comb (cresteria) is typical of classical Mayan architecture.

532–7 S. Sophia, ISTANBUL, TURKEY. Built by the Emperor Justinian in only six years, S. Sophia is the greatest of all Byzantine buildings.

690–92 Dome of the Rock, JERUSALEM, ISRAEL. The gold-domed shrine is the third most sacred in Islam after the Ka'aba at Mecca and the Mosque of the Prophet, Medina.

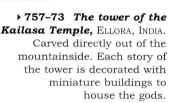

757–73 The tower of the Kailasa Temple, ELLORA, INDIA. Carved directly out of the mountainside. Each story of the tower is decorated with miniature buildings to house the gods.

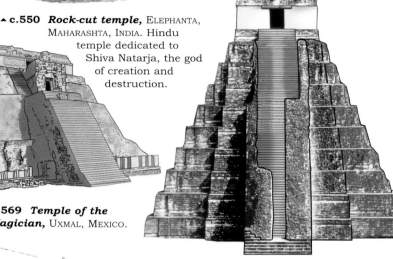

734 Temple II, TIKAL, GUATAMALA. Around AD830 the population of Tikal declined and their city was abandoned in the 10th century.

700–28 The Shore Temple, MAMALLAPURAM, TAMIL NADU, INDIA. Built by Nrisimhavarman II Rajasimha of finely dressed local granite and dedicated to the god Shiva Natarja.

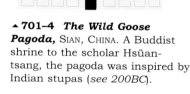

701–4 The Wild Goose Pagoda, SIAN, CHINA. A Buddist shrine to the scholar Hsüan-tsang, the pagoda was inspired by Indian stupas (see 200BC).

785 Interior of the Great Mosque, CORDOBA, SPAIN. Founded by 'Abd ar-Rahman I, the mosque is one of the most magnificent buildings of the Islamic tradition.

c.800 The Temple of Borobudar, JAVA. One of the most massive Buddhist shrines ever built. Pilgrims must circuit it nine times to reach the summit and its depiction of nirvana.

c.720 Palace at Yaxchilán, CHIAPAS, MEXICO.

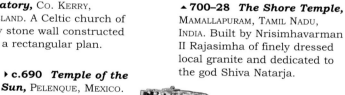

15 – TOGAS TO GO. The Huns introduce pants to the Roman empire, which replace traditional togas.

476 – WESTERN EMPIRE OF ROME COLLAPSES. Germanic and Slavic invaders overthrow the last emperor of Rome, Romulus Augustulus. Invaders claim the conquered territories.

527–565 – JUSTINIAN'S BYZANTIUM. The Byzantine Empire is at its height under Emperor Justinian I, famous for his laws, conquests, and the architecture constructed under his patronage.

BYZANTINE WOMAN

570 – MUHAMMAD IS BORN. The Prophet and founder of Islam born in Mecca, Arabia.

587 – JAPANESE BUDDHISM. The first Japanese Buddhist monastery is established.

618 – TANG DYNASTY BEGINS. Emperor Kao Zu founds the dynasty which brings a golden age to Chinese culture.

650 – THE KORAN IS WRITTEN. The sacred book of Islam is created by Muhammad's followers, containing the words revealed to the Prophet. The language is classic Arabic.

708 – TEA AND CHINA. By 708 tea becomes a popular beverage in China, both for its medicinal value and because it is safer to drink than untreated water.

800 – CHARLEMAGNE IS CROWNED. Charles the Great is anointed by the Pope on Christmas Day as the first emperor of what is later called the Holy Roman Empire.

Architect biographies

FILIPPO BRUNELLESCHI
1377–1446

"Of Filippo it may be said that he was given by Heaven to invest architecture with new forms..."

BRUNELLESCHI was born in Florence in 1377. He trained as a sculptor and goldsmith, becoming a master in 1404. He entered the famous design competition for the bronze doors of the Florence Baptistery, but lost to Ghiberti. Turning his attention to architecture, he found himself in competition with Ghiberti again, for the job of building the dome of Florence Cathedral (Santa Maria del Fiore). This time he won. Brunelleschi's solutions to the engineering challenge of building so vast a dome were groundbreaking and is still viewed as the first work of post-medieval architecture.

The innovations he used on the dome of Florence Cathedral (1417–34) were both technical and artistic. Brunelleschi pulled off a technical feat by building it without using temporary support. His secret weapon was a dome inside the dome – a self-supporting hemispherical dome that stayed in position inside the octagonal dome. On the exterior,

Ospidale degli Innocenti, Florence

the ribs become design elements, along with circular windows, architectural reliefs, and an elegant cupola.

In later works, like the unfinished Church of Santa Maria degli Angeli (1434–37), the Basilica of Santo Spirito (1434–82), and the Pazzi Chapel (1429–61), Brunelleschi shifted somewhat from the rigors of his geometric style. The Santa Maria design was highly significant as the first central-plan church of the Renaissance.

Brunelleschi was a pioneer in a milieu that was ripe for a break with the past. His genius was to take classical forms and create a whole new architectural idiom: one that quickly defined Renaissance style, and one that continues to influence architecture to this day.

LE CORBUSIER
1887–1965

LE CORBUSIER was the name adopted by Charles-Edouard Jeanneret to distinguish his architectural career from his early work as a painter. Jeanneret was born in 1887 in La Chaux-de-Fonds, Switzerland. He attended art school where he studied to be a watch engraver, like his father. As a young man he designed a series of houses for family and friends exhibiting a clear talent for architecture. After traveling throughout Europe and the Middle East, Jeanneret worked in Paris for the famous architect Auguste Perret, a pioneer in the architectural use of reinforced concrete. He also apprenticed in Germany in the office of Peter Behrens, a noted architect and industrial designer.

In 1917 he settled in Paris and soon became part of the intellectual and artistic community. Influenced by the work of Picasso and Braque, Jeanneret espoused a theory of art called Purism, which rejected perspective space. An important early commission for Le Corbusier was the house and studio he designed for his friend, the painter Ozenfant in Paris. Built at the same time as the publication of his first book *Vers une architecture,* (1923), translated as *'Toward a New Architecture'*, the building and the book set forth the principles that were the beginnings of the so called "international style" of modern architecture. The images which illustrated Le Corbusier's book were photographs of machines – cars, airplanes, and oceanliners. His memorable dictum, "the house is a machine for living" was embodied in the ship-like imagery of important early works. These include the Ozenfant Studio (1922); the house in Garches (a suburb of Paris) built for Gertrude Stein's brother (1927); and the extraordinary house built for Doctor Savoye at Poissy just outside Paris (1931).

Villa Savoye, Poissy

Le Corbusier also worked as a theoretical city planner. It is possible to argue that many of his built works were based on the components of his utopian city plans. In his book *Urbanisme* (1925) translated into English as 'The City of Tomorrow', Le Corbusier argued that it was the new city, clean, efficient, and built in a continuous park-like setting that would bring Europe into the 20th century and provide the 'good life' for its inhabitants. His continuing preoccupation with urbanism lead to his design for the Radiant City described in a book of the same name (La Ville Radieuse, 1933). His city plan, more like a zoning diagram than a formal plan, contained a catalogue of building types which were to dominate Le Corbusier's architectural production for the rest of his life. Most important among them was his *Unité* d'habitation in Marseilles (1946–52) a prototype housing block, raised off the ground on columns, containing an interior shopping street, a roof terrace, and balconies for each apartment. In the *Unité* each apartment was conceived as a duplex townhouse inserted into the unifying framework of the building's structural grid.

Le Corbusier's post-World War II architecture was markedly different from the machine aesthetic and painterly flatness of his early work. It was far more sculptural, primitive, and tactile in its use of exposed concrete. Le Corbusier's new exposed concrete buildings had an enormous impact on a younger generation of architects in England, America, and Japan, creating a style of architecture called the 'new brutalism.' Le Corbusier's most important works from this period were his pilgrimage chapel at Ronchamp, France (1953) and the city of Chandigarh in India (1950 to 1965).

The chapel at Ronchamp was the most poetic, intensely personal, and in some ways most enigmatic of Le Corbusier's later works. Sited on a hilltop that Le Corbusier compared to the Greek Acropolis, Ronchamp's ground plan is a transformation of a Latin cross church plan, while its roof shell, its dominant architectural element, relates to Le Corbusier's fascination with

tent structures and pavilions.

As an architectural innovator, Le Corbusier was a genius. He was an architect who painted, created furniture, wrote books and designed cities. While the development of his work embodied changing aesthetic ideas, it always reflected a singular world view, his belief that the built environment had the power to effect social change.

ANTONI GAUDÍ
1852–1926

"The straight line belongs to man, the curve to God." Gaudí

ANTONI GAUDÍ Y CORNET was born in 1852 in Reus, Spain, the son of a coppersmith. He began his training at the University of Barcelona in 1869, and designed his first major commission for the Casa Vicens (1878–85) in Barcelona. While the structure is fairly conventional, Gaudí put his stamp on it with brilliant multicolored tiling, elaborate ironwork, and striking neo-Moorish decoration.

Gaudí's sheer inventiveness began to assert itself with the Palau Guell (1885–89). This extraordinary building features a highly unusual entrance of two parabolic gateways and a rooftop of tile-encrusted chimneys and ventilators. Inside, the main room has the feel of a cavern – dark, spacious, and capped by a blue-tiled dome. In this period, Gaudí's embrace of Eastern forms met with another marked trend in his work: a devotion to natural forms. This is perhaps the most remarked-upon aspect of Gaudí's work. The Parc Guell (1900–14) is a no-holds-barred expression of Gaudí's love of naturalism. It was conceived as a 'garden city,' where snaking paths lead up to a forest of distorted Doric columns marking an area intended as a marketplace. Terrace benches are covered with dazzling broken mosaic work, as is the ceramic-clad roof of a porter's house. The complex is built from native stone, and the terrain's original contours were left unchanged.

The Casa Batlló (1904–06) and Casa Milá (1906–11] are high examples of Gaudí's naturalist bent, but also so much more in their uniqueness and, to many, downright bizarreness. Casa Batlló has been called the House of Bones, because its balconies appear to be made of the bones of mythical creatures while its façades are like the skin of a reptile. Casa Milá (*La Pedrera*) appears utterly organic. Its rounded façade seems to undulate like waves; its roof is topped by mysterious sculptural forms. The interior is emphatically curvilinear – not a right-angled room in the complex.

Casa Milá, Barcelona

Gaudí's masterwork, by his own reckoning, is the design of the Expiatory Church of the Sagrada Familia (1883–   ), which is not even

A–Z Architects

Latrobe, Benjamin Henry 1764–1820
• THE CAPITOL, Washington DC, from 1803
• BANK OF PENNSYLVANIA, Philadelphia, 1799–1801
• BALTIMORE CATHEDRAL, Baltimore, 1804–18
• EXCHANGE BUILDING, Baltimore, 1816–20
• (with Jefferson) UNIVERSITY OF VIRGINIA, 1817–26
• LOUISIANA STATE BANK, New Orleans, begun 1819.

Le Corbusier, see featured article.

Le Vau, Louis 1612–70
• HÔTEL LAMBERT, Paris, 1640–
• CHÂTEAU VAUX–LE–VICOMTE, 1657
• (with Lebrun) Rebuilt Galerie d'Apollon, Louvre, Paris, 1661–2
• REMODELING OF VERSAILLES, 1669
• COLLÈGE DES QUATRE NATIONS (now Institut de France), Paris, begun 1661.

Lemercier, Jacques 1585–1654
• LOUVRE EXTENSIONS, Paris, 1624
• PALAIS ROYAL, Paris, 1624–36
• CHURCH OF THE SORBONNE, Paris, France, begun 1626
• (with Perrault) PAVILLON DE L'HORLOGE, Louvre, Paris, completed 1641
• DOME, Val–de–Grâce, Paris, begun 1646.

Leonardo da Vinci, 1452–1519
• STUDIES FOR DOME and CROSSING, Milan Cathedral, 1487
• (with Bramante) CROSSING AND CHANCEL, SANTA MARIA DELLA GRAZIE, Milan, 1490s
• ROYAL RESIDENCE, Romoratin, France, c.1517–19.

Longhena, Baldassare c.1597–1682
• PALAZZO GIUSTINIAN-LOLIN, Venice, 1620–3
• S.MARIA DELLA SALUTE, Venice, begun 1630
• DOUBLE STAIRCASE, monastery of S. Giorgio Maggiore, Venice, 1643–5
• PALAZZO REZZONICO, Venice, begun 1667
• PALACE, Pesaro,Venice, 1649–82
• OSPEDALETTO, Venice, 1670–78.

Loos, Adolf 1870–1933
• Steiner House, Vienna, 1910
• Tristan Tzara House, Paris, 1925
  Müller House, Prague, 1928.

McKim White & Mead,
Charles Follen McKim (1847–1909);
William Rutherford Mead (1846–1928);
Stanford White (1853–1906)
• VILLARD MANSIONS, New York, 1882–5
• WILLIAM G. LOWE HOUSE, Bristol, Rhode Island, 1886–7
• BOSTON PUBLIC LIBRARY, 1887–8
• RHODE ISLAND STATE CAPITOL, 1891–1903
• COLUMBIA UNIVERSITY, New York, 1893–4
• PIERPONT MORGAN LIBRARY, New York, 1902–7
• METROPOLITAN MUSEUM OF ART, New York, 1906.

Melnikov, Konstantin 1890–1974
• SOVIET PAVILION, Paris Exposition, 1925
• RUSAKOV WORKERS' CLUB, Moscow, 1927
• MELNIKOV HOUSE, Moscow, 1927.

Mies Van der Rohe, see featured article.

Michelangelo, Buonarotti, 1475–1564
• EXTERIOR OF CHAPEL of Pope Leo X, Rome, 1513–21
• MEDICI CHAPEL, Florence, 1519–34
• BIBLIOTECA LAURENZIANA, Florence, 1524–71
• LIBRARY FOR SAN LORENZO, Florence, 1526
• REORGANIZATION OF THE CAPITOL, Rome, begun 1539
• COMPLETED PALAZZO FARNESE, Rome, begun 1546
• SFORZA CHAPEL, S.Maria Maggiore, Rome, completed 1560
• REMODELING SANTA MARIA DEGLI ANGELI, Rome, 1561
• ST PETER'S, Rome, 1546–64.

Nash, John 1752–1835
• RAVENSWORTH CASTLE, Ireland, 1808
• REGENT'S PARK terraces, 1819
• BRIGHTON PAVILION, 1815–21
• HAYMARKET THEATRE, London, 1820–21
• ALL SOUL'S LANGHAM SQUARE, London, 1822–5
• UNITED SERVICES CLUB, London, 1826–8
• CARLTON HOUSE TERRACE, London, 1827–33.

Nervi, Pier Luigi 1891–32
• STADIUM, Florence, 1930–32
• EXHIBITION HALL, Turin, 1948
• (with Breuer) UNESCO BUILDING, Paris, 1953–6
• (with Ponti) PIRELLI SKYSCRAPER, Milan, 1955–8
• (with Piacentini) PALAZZETTO DELLO SPORT, Rome, 1960.

Neumann, Johann Balthasar 1687–1753
• RESIDENZ, Würzberg, begun 1719
• STAIRCASE, Schlöss Augustusburg, Brühl, 1740–8
• PILGRIMAGE CHURCH, Gössweinstein, 1729–39
• COLLEGIATE CHURCH OF ST PAULINIUS, Trier, 1734–54
• PILGRIMAGE CHURCH, Vierzehnheiligen, Germany, 1742–53
• BENEDICTINE ABBEY CHURCH, Neresheim, 1745–92
• MARIENKIRCHE, Limbach, 1747–52.

Neutra, Richard Josef 1892–1970
• DR LOVELL HEALTH HOUSE, Los Angeles, 1929
• KAUFMANN HOUSE, Palm Springs, 1947.

Niemeyer, Oscar, born 1907
• BRAZILIAN PAVILION, New York World Fair, 1939
• CASINO, CLUB, AND SÃO FRANCISCO CHAPEL, Pamtulhe, Brazil, 1942–3
• PRESIDENT'S PALACE, Supreme Court, Cathedral, Government Buildings, Brazilia, 1958–70
• APARTMENTS FOR INTERBAU EXHIBITION, Berlin, 1957
• MONDADORI BUILDING, Milan, 1968–76.

Palladio, see featured article.

Paxton, Sir Joseph 1803–65
• EDENSOR VILLAGE, Derbyshire, 1838–48
• CRYSTAL PALACE, London, 1850–51
• MENTMORE TOWERS, Buckinghamshire, 1851–4.

Pei, Ieoh Ming b.1917
• MILE HIGH CENTER, Denver, Colorado, 1952–6
• (with Affleck) PLACE VILLE MARIE, Montreal, 1956–65
• EAST WING, National Gallery of Art, Washington DC, 1971–8
• MERTON H. MYERSON SYMPHONY CENTER, Dallas, 1981–9
• BANK OF CHINA, Hong Kong, 1982–9
• LOUVRE EXTENSION, Paris, 1983–93.

Perrault, Claude 1613–88
• (with La Vau and Lebrun) EAST FRONT OF LOUVRE, Paris, begun 1665–74
• OBSERVATOIRE, Paris, 1667.

Porta, Giacomo della c.1533–1602
• PALAZZO DEI SENATORI, Rome, 1573–1602
• FAÇADE OF IL GESÙ, Rome, 1571–84
• NORTH AND SOUTH FOUNTAINS, Piazza Navona, Rome, 1574–8
• WESTERN ARM AND MINOR DOME, St Peter's, Rome, 1586–92
• (with Fontana) MAIN DOME, St Peter's, Rome, 1588–90
• PALAZZO DELLA SAPIENZA, Rome, completed 1575
• S. MARIA AI MORTI, Rome, begun 1580
• PALAZZO MARESCOTTI, Rome, completed 1590
• VILLA ALDOBRANDINI, Frascati, 1594–1603.

Pugin, Augustus Welby Northmore 1812–52
• (with Barry) PALACE OF WESTMINSTER, London, 1840–70
• ST. GILES, Cheadle, Staffordshire, 1841–6
• ST. BARNABAS'S CATHEDRAL, Nottingham, 1841–4
• ST AUGUSTINE, Ramsgate, 1843–52

Raphael, Rafaello Sanzio 1483–1520
• SANT'EGLIO DEGLI OREFICI, Rome, begun 1511
• PALAZZO PANDOLFINI, Florence, 1517
• PALAZZO BRESCIANO, Rome, completed 1515
• PALAZZO BRANCONIA DELL'AQUILA, Rome, 1513
• CHIGI CHAPEL IN S.MARIA DEL POPOLO, Rome, begun 1512

Rastrelli, Bartolomeo Francesco 1700–71
• BIRON PALACE, Latvia, 1736–40
• ST. ANDREAS CHURCH, Kiev, 1747–67
• VORONTSOV AND STROGANOV PALACES, St Petersburg, 1750s
• SMOLNY CATHEDRAL AND CONVENT, St Petersburg, 1748–57
• GRAND PALACE, Tsarskoe Selo, 1749–59
• WINTER PALACE, St Petersburg, 1754–62.

Richardson, Henry Hobson 1838–86
• BRATTLE SQUARE CHURCH, Boston, 1871–3
• TRINITY CHURCH, Boston, 1873–7
• MEMORIAL LIBRARY, Woburn, Mass., 1876–9
• WATTS SHERMAN HOUSE, Newport, Rhode Island, 1874–5
• MARSHALL FIELD WAREHOUSE, Chicago, 1885–7
• GLESSNER HOUSE, Chicago, 1885–7
• SEVER HOUSE, Cambridge, Mass. 1882–3.

Rogers, Lord Richard b.1937
• CENTRE POMPIDOU, Paris, 1971–77
• FLEETGUARD FACTORY, Quimper, France, 1979
• LLOYDS BUILDING, London, 1978–86

Saarinen, Eero 1910–61
• GENERAL MOTORS TECHNICAL CENTER, Warren, Michigan, 1947–56
• KRESGE AUDITORIUM AND MEMORIAL CHAPEL, Massachusetts Institute Of Technology, 1952–6
• DAVID S. INGALLS ICE HOCKEY RINK, Yale University, New Haven, Connecticut, 1953–9
• TWA TERMINAL, Kennedy Airport, New York, 1956–62
• EZRA STILES & MORSE COLLEGES, Yale University, New Haven, Connecticut, 1958–62
• DULLES INTERNATIONAL AIRPORT, Washington DC, 1958–63
• US EMBASSY, London, 1955–60.

Sansovino, Jacopo d'Antonio Tatti 1486–1570
• PALAZZO GADDI, Rome, 1518
• ZECCA (Mint), Venice, 1535–45
• BIBLIOTECA MARCIANA, Venice, begun 1537
• LOGIETTA, Venice, 1537–42
• PALAZZO CORNER DELLA CA'GRANDE, Venice, begun 1537
• S.FRANCESCO della VIGNA, Venice, 1534
• FAÇADE OF S. GIULIANO, Venice, 1553–5
• VILLA GARZONI, Pontecasale, 1535–45.

Schinkel, Karl Friedrich 1781–1841
• NEUE WACHE, Berlin, Germany, 1816–18
• SCHAUSPIELHAUS, Berlin, Germany, 1818–21
• ALTES MUSEUM, Berlin, Germany, 1824–30
• FREIDRICHWERDERSCHKIRCHE, Berlin, Germany, 1824–7
• NIKOLAIKIRCHE, Potsdam, Germany, 1830–7
• BAUAKADEMIE, Berlin, Germany, 1831–6

Scott, Sir George Gilbert 1811–78
• CHAPEL OF EXETER COLLEGE, Oxford University, 1856
• ST. JOHN'S COLLEGE, Cambridge University, 1863–9
• PARISH CHURCH KENSINGTON, London, 1869–72
• KELHAM HALL, Nottinghamshire, begun 1857
• ST. PANCRAS STATION HOTEL, London, 1868–74
• ALBERT MEMORIAL, London, 1863–72
• GLASGOW UNIVERSITY BUILDINGS, begun 1868
• WAR AND FOREIGN OFFICE, London, 1862–73

Shaw, Richard Norman 1831–1912
• HOLY TRINITY, Bingley, Yorkshire, 1864–8
• LEYS WOOD, Sussex, 1868
• GRIM'S DYKE, Harrow Weald, 1870–72
• NEW ZEALAND CHAMBERS, London, 1871–3
• LOWTHER LODGE, London, 1873
• NEW SCOTLAND YARD, London, 1887–90
• PICCADILLY HOTEL, London, 1905

Sinan, see featured article.

Skidmore, Owings & Merrill,
Louis Skidmore (1897–1962);
Nathaniel Owings (1903–84);
John Ogden Merrill (1896–1975)
• LEVER HOUSE, New York, 1952
• CHASE MANHATTAN BANK, New York, 1952–4
• US AIR FORCE ACADEMY, Colorado Springs, begun 1955
• INLAND STEEL BUILDING, Chicago, 1958
• PEPSI COLA BUILDING, New York, 1960
• JOHN HANCOCK CENTER, Chicago, 1970
• NINE WEST 57TH STREET, New York, 1972
• SEARS TOWER, Chicago, 1974
• NATIONAL COMMERCIAL BANK, Jeddah, Saudi Arabia,1982
• CANARY WHARF, London, 1990.

Smythson, Robert c.1535–1614
• LONGLEAT HOUSE,Wiltshire, 1550–80
• WOLLATON HALL, Nottinghamshire, 1568–72
• MONTACUTE HOUSE, Somerset, 1588–1601
• HARDWICK HALL, Derbyshire, 1590–97.

Soufflot, Jacques–Germain 1713–80
• HÔTEL–DIEU, Lyons, 1739–48
• THÉÂTRE, Lyons, 1753–6
• PANTHÉON, Paris, begun 1757
• ECÔLE DE DROIT, Paris, begun 1771.

Sullivan, Louis Henry 1856–1924
• (with Adler) AUDITORIUM BUILDING, Chicago, 1886–90
• CARSON, PIRIE, SCOTT & CO, Chicago, 1899–1904
• (with Adler) ANSHE MAARIV SYNAGOGUE, Chicago, 1890
• GARRICK THEATER, Chicago, 1892
• (with Adler) STOCK EXCHANGE, Chicago, 1893–4
• (with Adler) GUARANTY BUILDING, Buffalo, 1894–5
• (with Adler) WAINWRIGHT BUILDING, St Louis, 1894
• BAYARD (Condict) BUILDING, New York, 1898
• NATIONAL FARMER'S BANK, Owatonna, Minnesota, 1907–8.

Vanbrugh, Sir John 1664–1726
• CASTLE HOWARD, Yorkshire, 1699–1712
• BLENHEIM PALACE, Oxfordshire, 1705–24
• KIMBOLTON CASTLE, Huntingdonshire, 1707–10
• KING'S WESTON, Gloucestershire, 1710–19
• SEATON DELAVAL, Northumberland, 1720–8.

Vasari, Giorgio 1511–74
• UFFIZZI, Florence, begun, 1560
• SS. FIORA E LUCILLA, Arezzo, begun 1566
• LOGGIA, Piazza Grande, Venice, 1570–96.

Vauban, Sébastien le Prestre de 1633–1707
• FORTIFICATIONS, Lille, 1668–74
• FORTIFICATIONS, Maubeuge, 1683–5
• FORTIFICATIONS, Neuf-Brisach, 1697–1708.

Vignola, Giacomo Barozzi da 1507–73
• VILLA GIULIA, Rome, 1551–5
• PALAZZO FARNESE, Caprarola, 1559
• S. ANNA DEI PALAFRENIERI, Rome, 1565
• IL GESÙ, Rome, 1568
• PALAZZO FARNESE, Piacenza, 1558
• ARCHITECT TO ST PETER'S, Rome, 1567–73.

Viollet–le–Duc, Eugène–Emmanuel 1814–79
• RESTORATION, Sainte Chapelle, Paris, begun 1840
• RESTORATION, NOTRE DAME, Paris, 1844–64
• RESTORATION, CARCASSONNE, begun 1844
• RESTORATION, CHÂTEAU DE PIERREFONDS, 1858–70.

Waterhouse, Alfred 1830–1905
• TOWN HALL, Manchester, 1869–77
• NATURAL HISTORY MUSEUM, London, 1873–81
• ST PAUL'S SCHOOL, London, 1881–4
• NATIONAL LIBERAL CLUB, London, 1885–7.

Wren see featured article.

Wright see featured article.

ELEVENTH CENTURY

▲ c.1000 *Lingaraja Temple,* BHUBANESHWAR, ORISSA, INDIA. Unlike Muktesvara (*see AD950*) the decoration here is strictly subordinate to structure.

▲ 836 *The minaret of the Great Mosque of Kairoan,* TUNISIA. This type of minaret may have been based on ancient lighthouses like the one at Alexandria.

◄ 842 *S. Maria de Naranco,* OVIEDO, SPAIN. A unique Visigothic church with two rectangular halls, one above the other.

▲ c.1000 *The Castillo,* CHICHÉN ITZÁ, MEXICO. Each stairway has 91 steps making 364 total, with the sanctuary threshold at the top making 365 – the solar year.

▲ c.1040 *St Mark's,* VENICE, ITALY. Venice owed more to the Byzantine world than to western Europe and St Mark's is one of the glories of Byzantine style. The present building is the third on this site and became the Cathedral of Venice in 1481.

◄ c.1055 *'Enemy Observation Pagoda',* K'AI YUAN TEMPLE, HOPEI, CHINA. Built of solid brick but without floors or staircases it was purely decorative despite its war-like name.

▼ 1066–1338 *Tourn Cathedral,* BELGIUM. Nave (*righ* is Romanesque; t transepts (*cente* are Transition the Choir (*left*) Goth

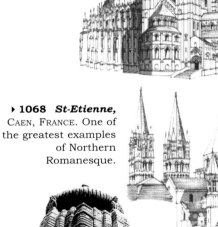

◄ 1019–47 *Trier Cathedral,* GERMANY. The present Romanesque building incorporates a Roman temple that preceded it.

▸ 1068 *St-Etienne,* CAEN, FRANCE. One of the greatest examples of Northern Romanesque.

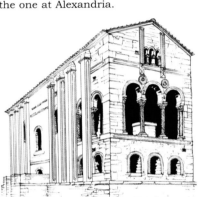

▲ c.850 *The Little Metropole Cathedral,* ATHENS, GREECE. Byzantine churches in Greece tended to be smaller and simpler than their counterparts in Constantinople (modern Istanbul).

▸ c.1075 *Rajarani Templ* BHUBANESHWAR, INDIA. The tower (*rekha deul*) is flanke by a lower ritual dance pavilion (*jagamohana*).

▲ c.851 *The Great Mosque of Susah,* TUNISIA. The fortified mosque was built by the Aghlabids by remodeling an ancient kasbah that had originally been used to repel the invading Byzantines. The domed structure (technically known as a 'kiosk') dates from the 11th century.

▲ c.1020 *Abbey Church of Mont-St-Michel,* FRANCE. Although founded in the 8th century, the present Norman Romanesque buildings date from the early 11th century.

808 – FEZ IS MORE THAN A HAT. Abbasid King Idris establishes the city of Fez in Morocco, which becomes the cultural center of North Africa.

867 – MACEDONIAN DYNASTY TAKES ROOT. Byzantine Emperor Basil I establishes the dynasty that will rule Byzantium until 1054.

868 – PUBLISHING IN CHINA. The Diamond Sutra, produced in China, becomes the world's first printed book.

899 – ALFRED THE GREAT DIES. England's ruler dies after neutralizing the threat of the Danes, consolidating English power, codifying laws, and advancing learning.

910 – ABBEY OF CLUNY IS FOUNDED. France's premier monastery will soon become one of the wealthiest and most powerful in Europe.

975 – SIMPLIFYING NUMBERS. Arabic arithmetical notation is introduced to Europe, making calculating easier than when using Roman numerals.

988 – RUSSIA AND CHRISTIANITY. Kiev's grand duke Vladimir converts to Christianity, marries the Emperor's sister Anna, and begins a general conversion of Russia.

999 – JUDGMENT DAY. Christians across Europe fear the end of the world at the turn of the millennium. When it doesn't come, they build churches in gratitude for being spared.

A FEMALE COMMONER

EUROPEAN ARMOR 1075

1066 – NORMAN CONQUEST OF ENGLAND. William, duke of Normandy, defeats England's Anglo-Saxon king, Harold II, at the Battle of Hastings. William captures London and becomes the first Norman king of England.

THIRTEENTH CENTURY

1200   **1250**   **1300**

◄ **c.1200** *Torres Meliandi* (left) and *Rognosa,* SAN GIMINIANO, ITALY. Look-out towers, defenses, drying towers for the town's famous saffron-dyed wool – or just one-upmanship between wealthy families?

► **c.1221** *Burgos Cathedral,* SPAIN. Like the cathedrals of León and Toledo, Burgos was based on French models and was built by French and English master-masons. The spires and pinnacles are 15–16th century additions.

◄ **1280** *Halles,* BRUGES, BELGIU An imposing statement of the ci wealth from cloth manufacture during the Middle Ages. The tow is 260ft (80m) high.

▼ **c.1200** *Cliff Palace,* MESA VERDE, CANYON DE CHELLY, COLORADO, USA. The Pueblo Indians had occupied this site since c.AD300, but the present buildings date from the early thirteenth century. They exploited the natural caves and fissures in the cliff face by excavating the soft sandstone, then added more rooms and storage areas with sandstone blocks cemented together with mud-and-water (*adobe*) mortar.

◄ **1227** *Toledo Cathedral,* SPAIN. "Clothed in russet tones, the color of a browning roast or of a skin tanned like that of a pilgrim from Palestine."

▼ **1283–1383** *Caernavon Castle,* WALES. The grandest the 'golden age' of English castles built king Edward I (reign 1272–1307). There a 13 towers, none of them identical.

◄ **1288–1309** *Palazzo Pubblico,* SIENA, ITALY. Mediev Italy produced a wealth of tow halls – the centers of government of the city-states. Siena's, with its imposing tow castellated roofline, and Goth windows, is typical.

▼ **c.1200** *S. Millán,* SEGOVIA, SPAIN. The most unusual of the three Romanesque churches in Segovia, S. Millán has a striking arcaded entrance.

► **1245** *Siena Cathedral,* ITALY. Clad all over in dramatic alternating stripes of black and white marble, it is also further embellished with mosaic, bronze sculpture and marble veneer.

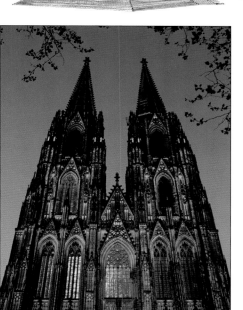

► **1296** *Fountain,* IBN TULUN MOSQUE, CAIRO, EGYPT. In the center of the great mosque is a dome-covered fountain, almost a shrine to that sacred element in Egypt – water.

◄ **1220–1380** *Salisbury Cathedral,* ENGLAND. A perfect example of Early English style. The foundation stone was laid in 1220 and the Lady Chapel completed by 1225. The east transepts and choir were finished by 1237; the nave by 1284, and the tower and spire about 1380.

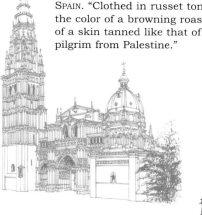

◄ **1248** *Cologne Cathedral,* GERMANY. The largest Gothic cathedral in northern Europe – the vault of the nave alone could contain Beauvais cathedral!

► **c.1300** *Timber house,* SØR-FRON, NORWAY. Most building in Norway at this time was in timber as stone and brick were scarce and expensive. Cloth or moss was laid between the logs to make the walls air- and water-tight.

1200   **1250**   **1300**

1202 – COMEDY COMES TO COURT. The first court jesters appear in Europe.

1209 – THE FRANCISCANS ORGANIZE. The Franciscan order begins when Giovanni Francesco Bernardone (later St. Francis of Assisi) obtains approval for a rule from Pope Innocent III.

ENTERTAINER

1211 – GENGHIS KHAN INVADES CHINA. The supreme ruler of the Mongol Empire continues to conquer lands to the east and west of Central Asia.

1215 – THE MAGNA CARTA IS SIGNED. King John of England sets his seal to the Magna Carta at Runnymede.

1222 – RUSSIA MEETS GENGHIS KHAN. The warrior's invasion of Russia is his first incursion into Europe.

1225 – COTTON COMES TO SPAIN. Cotton begins to be manufactured in Spain, competing with wool and linen.

1240 – ALEKSANDR NEVSKI PREVAILS. Prince Aleksandr of Novgorod defeats Swedish forces on the banks of the Neva River. He is called Aleksandr Nevski from then on.

1271 – MARCO POLO MAKES HIS MOVE. The great explorer leaves Venice to journey to India and China.

1282 – FLORENCE FLOURISHES. Florence, Italy is the dominant European center of commerce and finance.

COMMONER

1315 – LEARNING ANATOMY. The first public, systematic dissection of a human corpse is overseen by Italian surgeon Mondino de Luzzi. Luzzi will later publish Anatomia.

ENGLISH OFFICIAL

1070 The White Tower, Tower of London, England. The Normans introduced strong stone keeps or donjons (rectangular towers) which could serve as living quarters for the noble family and its retinue. Other examples are Loches and Langeais in France (c.1080) and Dover, England (1181–87).

1150 Krak des Chevaliers, Syria, a Crusader castle built by the Knights of St John (Knights Hospitallers) has been called "the best preserved and most wholly admirable castle in the world." It withstood prolonged sieges by the Muslims until 1271.

1170–82 Saladin builds the great citadel of Old Cairo, among the finest works of military architecture of the medieval period.

▾ 1180 Gravensteen Castle, Ghent, Belgium. Built by Philip of Alsace, Count of Flanders.

▾ 1196–8 Richard I (Lionheart) completes the construction of Château Gaillard, France, incorporates many of the lessons he had learned during the Third Crusade. Gaillard was one of the most formidable castles of its day.

c.1200 Round keeps begin to replace rectangular. Tour de César, Provins and Etampes, in France; Conisborough and Orford in England are fine examples.

▾ 1230 Eilean Donan Castle, Scotland. A fortress for the Macrae clan.

▾ 1247 Carcassonne, France. The old walls (dating from Roman and Visigothic times) were strongly reinforced with the addition of an outer curtain wall, towers and gatehouses.

▴ 1310 Among the finest military works of the 14th century are the fortifications of the citadel of Rhodes, built by the Knights of St John. It was forced to capitulate in 1523 after a prolonged siege by Suleiman the Magnificent.

▾ 1308–80 Ponte Valentré, Cahors, France. A fine example of a medieval fortified bridge.

Caernarvon

◂ 1272–1307 Edward I, king of England. During his pacification of Wales Edward built a string of formidable castles which, because they were never tested in war, remain today almost intact.

Harlech

Conway

1370–83 The Bastille, Paris. One of the most powerful fortifications of its time. Destroyed during the French Revolution.

▴ 1386–90 Bodiam Castle, England.

▴ 1390–1400 Château de Pierrefonds, France. Protected on three sides by natural escarpements and on the fourth by outworks. The towers and walls are all defended by machicolated parapets (stone overhangs that allowed defenders to drop burning material or stones down on to attackers).

▴ 1488 Amsterdamsche Poort, Haarlem, Holland. The gateways to medieval towns were often heavily defended and also served as customs points at which taxes were collected on imported goods.

A Penthouse address

The origin of the term pent house derives from the Roman covered passage (*musculus*), made of timber and covered in hide and tiles, used to protect soldiers while they were undermining the walls of a besieged fortress or town.

▴ 1594 Matsumoto Castle, Nagano, Japan. Many of the finest castles in Japan were built during the Momoyama period (1573–1638). Matsumoto is typical in standing on a stone base (*glacis*) that is surrounded by a moat. The keep was wooden.

17th century Sébastian le Prestre de Vauban (1633–1707) was commissioned by Louis XIV of France to build a series of forts (the Pré Carré) on the frontier with the then Spanish Netherlands. His moated star-shaped fortresses left no 'blind spots' where an attacker could hide. Defenders could fire on the enemy with cannon protected by thick walls and rake the moats with handguns fired through slits in the walls. During his career he built 33 forts and strengthened 300 others throughout France.

▾ 1869–81 Neuschwanstein, Bavaria. The castle as romantic fantasy. Designed by Eduard Reidel (1813–85) and Georg von Dollmann (1830–95) for Ludwig II of Bavaria.

1929 André Maginot, French Minister for War, starts building the ill-fated Maginot line: a system of 50 forts stretching from the Belgian border in the west to the Swiss border in the east. When Germany attacked France in 1940 key forts were either knocked out by German special forces teams, or simply by-passed.

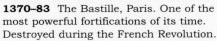

Introduction

A building is not only a structure.
It is spirit made manifest.

The *Architecture Timecharts* is not meant to be a comprehensive history of human building; the limitations of space prohibit that. But it does set out to show representative types of building from different parts of the world at any given time in history. Many of the buildings included here are world famous while others are humbler, vernacular, structures that serve to put the grander edifices in context. They also serve to underline the continuity of building traditions. For example, the Idlib mud huts of Iraq or the Mongolian yurt are still being constructed today pretty much as they were thousands of years ago.

By taking the comparative world view it is fascinating to put Western European architecture in context. For example, The Temple of the Magician at Uxmal on the Yucatan peninsula of Mexico was constructed at about the same time as the great Christian Byzantine church of S. Sophia in Istanbul; the Iroqouis longhouse of the Woodland Indians of eastern North America sitting next in time to the Duomo in Florence, or Machu Picchu in Peru standing alongside some of the great Loire châteaux like Chambord and Chenonceaux. The concertina panorama which forms part of this book gives a dramatic 'at-a-glance' survey of these juxtapositions.

The object of *The Architecture Timecharts* is to make us aware of the history of architecture throughout the world, and in so doing break the mold of many introductions to the history of architecture that are Euro-centric and focus only on 'great' buildings.

Dating

Sometimes we can discern from the records when a building was constructed, but in many cases there is inadequate or confusing evidence. A building may be planned but not immediately executed. Or it may be planned but take centuries to complete, with many changes of personnel. The medieval cathedrals of western Europe are a good example. Let us look at the progression of just one of the greatest, Durham Cathedral, England:

1093–99	*Choir*
1099–1128	*Nave*
1128–33	*Nave vault*
1133–40	*Chapter House*
c.1170	*Galilee*
c.1220	*West towers (upper stages)*
1242–80	*Chapel of Nine Altars*
c.1341	*West window*
1366–71	*Kitchen*
1375–80	*Reredos (Neville screen)*
1390–1418	*Cloisters*
1465–75	*Central tower (lower stage)*
c.1483–90	*Central tower (upper stage)*

On the other hand, the great church of S. Sophia, Constantinople (modern Istanbul) was built for the Emperor Justinian in an amazingly fast time between AD532 and 537.

In some cultures, notably Japan and China, ancient buildings were reconstructed on the same pattern over and over again down through the centuries. The culture was less interested in innovation than it was in continuity, and the building materials themselves, mainly wood, allowed for this kind of renovation.

Style is not always as clear a guide as one might imagine. The neat academic delineations between, say, Carolingian, Romanesque and Gothic, turn out to be shifting boundaries. Different regions not only adopted styles at varying times but they also adapted them to their own needs and taste.

The dates we give here are either start date (or completion when noted) and, where possible, the span of time from start to finish.

The Architect

To construct is to collaborate. The complexity of buildings has to involve teams of specialists. Although we know the name of the architect of one of the earliest structures recorded here – the Step Pyramid of Zoser at Saqqara in Egypt, built by the pharaoh Zoser's chief minister and architect, Imhotep, in about 2778BC – many architects of Antiquity and the Middle Ages are, if not anonymous, known by different titles than we would recognize today. We know the names of a medieval patron like Abbot Suger of St Denis

A medieval master mason, with square and rule, oversees his craftsmen.

in France, for example, and we may know the names of many of the stonemasons and craftsmen of the great medieval European cathedrals but the 'architect', the central guiding hand, was most probably a master-mason like Villard de Honnencourt whose 13th century sketchbooks (now in the Bibliothèque Nationale, Paris) cover the wide range of subjects a medieval 'architect' was meant to master: mechanics, geometry, trigonometry, architectural design, plans, elevations, sections, designs for ornaments, figures, and furniture. He was head of all the workmen, priced the materials, and was responsible for the administrative duties of the Clerk of the Works, but his principal duties were to provide plans and elevations which were often drawn on parchment documents which, because they were precious commodities, would be cleaned and reused for subsequent buildings – hence the great scarcity of medieval plans. In recognition of his skill he was paid three or four times as much as a skilled craftsman, and often even had his likeness carved on his buildings.

It was not until the Renaissance that the architect began to take on the modern sense of 'author' of a building. But even then, many 'architects' looked on their building work as an extension or addition to other accomplishments. Like Imhotep (who was a courtier, priest, and man of medicine) many architects prided themselves on their multi-faceted achievements. Raphael and Pietro da Cortona saw themselves primarily as painters; Michelangelo and Bernini as sculptors; Bramante a poet and sculptor; Wren and Guarini as mathematicians; Vanbrugh as a soldier and playwright.

Often great buildings had many architects involved over time. Take St. Peter in Rome as an example. In 1503 Pope Julius II decided to replace the ancient basilica of St Peter and commissioned Bramante to design a new building. The Pope laid the first stone in 1506 but Bramante died in 1514. Between 1514 and 1547 (when Michelangelo took over and worked on it until his death in 1564) several other architects were involved: Peruzzi, Giuliano da Sangallo, Raphael, and Antonio da Sangallo. The dome was completed in 1587–90 by Giacomo della Porta and Domenico Fontana.

AN OVERVIEW

Our prehistoric forebears were nomadic hunter-gatherers living in caves or temporary shelters made of hide-covered branches or transportable tent-like dwellings perhaps similar to the yurt. It was around 8000BC that the first agricultural revolution took place and small farms and agricultural communities were established in what are now Iran and Iraq. No longer itinerant, they had a need for permanent buildings to live in, to store food, and to protect themselves from raiders.

Their main building material was sun-dried bricks made of mud or clay and the houses they built were square or rectangular with either a flat or pitched wooden-beam roof covered with straw and sealed with clay. Mud bricks do not last long, and as houses were degraded by weather they were simply leveled and new ones built on the site reusing as much of the original material as was salvageable.

The Great Ziggurat of Ur, Iraq, c.2125BC.

The world's first monumental structures were built by the Sumerians of Mesopotamia around 3500BC. They were temples, usually perched on the top of ziggurats – stepped mounds built of dried mud brick reinforced with reeds and bitumen. It is fascinating to see from the earliest beginnings of monumental building an almost universal spiritual need to reach up to the heavens. The specific gods may change through history but the ambition remains constant.

Egypt

The founding of the First Dynasty in 3100BC marks the beginning of Egyptian civilization as we usually conceive it. In the Third Dynasty, about 2770BC, Pharaoh Zoser commissioned his first minister and chief engineer, Imhotep, to build a magnificent funerary step-pyramid at Saqqara. Imhotep is generally recognized as the first named architect in history, as well as being the first to build with cut stone.

Prior to this architectural watershed, royal tombs had been fairly modest affairs, low flat-topped brick boxes called mastaba. Imhotep superimposed one mastaba-type box on the other until he had six levels reaching up 66m/200ft.

The Fourth Dynasty (2615–2494BC) was the great age of pyramid building. The three most significant are clustered on the Nile on the outskirts of what is now Cairo. The largest was

The pyramids of Giza, Egypt, c. 2500BC.

built for Pharaoh Khufu (Cheops in Greek) by the architect/engineer Hemon. The base is 571,000 square feet /63,000 square meters rising to 500ft/166m and constructed of 2.5 million blocks of dressed stone, each weighing 2.5 tons/tonnes. For nearly 5000 years it was the tallest building in the world.

By 2000BC the political center of Egypt had moved up the Nile to Thebes where vast temples were built. The most famous, the Temple of Amon at Karnak (completed c.1300 BC) has a hypostyle hall, a large room with a flat roof supported by multiple rows of columns.

The temple of Amon, Karnak, Egypt, c.100BC.

Greece

The 2nd millennium BC saw more monumental building on the island of Crete, most spectacularly the 'Palace of King Minos' at Knossos, which was destroyed about 1400BC and never rebuilt (what we see now is a rather crude

ABOVE: The palace of Knossos, Crete, c. 1600BC.

BELOW: The Lion Gate, citadel of Mycenae, Greece, c.1350BC

reconstruction).

Minoan civilization spread to the Greek mainland and a new culture grew there centered on Mycenae on the Peloponnese. The citadel of Mycenae (close to the present day port of Nauplia) was rebuilt about 1350BC and the lion carving on the main gateway is the most ancient carved sculpture in Europe. About 1100BC the Mycenaen settlements were destroyed by invaders from the north but their legacy was inherited by the Hellenic Greeks several centuries later.

Hellenic Greece c.700–146BC

The Greeks were a maritime civilization and much influenced by their contacts with Egypt, Assyria, and Persia. Greek Doric Order, the most important of the Orders for the Hellenic Greeks, has something of Egyptian monumentality about it. Color was important to them and we tend to forget how richly painted were both their interiors and exteriors because most of it has been lost.

It is also difficult to get a sense of the living buildings from the ruins left to us, none of which is intact. The sculpture has been shipped to museums, the roofs are gone, the wood and metal elements destroyed by time. The Greeks (like the Japanese and Chinese) were not particularly interested in innovation for its own sake. Their concern was to work intensively on established forms, perfecting proportion and line to create an overwhelming harmony.

Greek architecture belongs to three main eras: the Archaic (c.700–480BC); Early Classical (c.480–200BC), and Later Hellenic (c.200–146BC when Greece was absorbed by the Roman Empire).

The system of Orders that the ancient Greeks devised had a profound effect on European architecture right up to our own time. Each Order (Doric, Ionic, Corinthian) consisted of a column with a base (optional) and a capital that

The Parthenon, Athens, Greece, c.447–436BC.

supported a horizontal slab called the entablature. Each Order had its own specific relative proportions between the parts, which remained fixed no matter what the scale. The Greeks rarely used more than one Order on any single building. Simplicity and restraint were guiding principles.

The most important form was the temple which was built to house an effigy of the deity rather than being a house of congregation as in the Christian, Jewish, and Islamic traditions. In this it performed a similar function to the temples of India and the Oriental East where worshippers walked around the temple rather than gathered in it to worship.

All temples were raised on a platform (*stylobate*) with an entrance door placed in the center of a wall behind a colonnaded porch (*portico*). Inside there was little natural light, and what there was was directed on to the statue of the

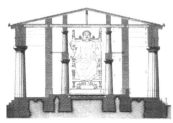

Temple of Zeus (reconstruction), Olympia, Greece, c. 460BC.

deity. For example, the Parthenon of Athens (c.447–432BC) housed a 40ft/13m statue of the goddess Athena made of gold and ivory. The whole effect was designed to create a theatrical, dramatic atmosphere, a characteristically Greek interweaving of theater and religion.

Rome: 753BC–c.AD400

The tribal settlement that was established on the Palatine Hill in Rome on the banks of the river Tiber in 753BC is traditionally accepted as the beginning of Roman civilization (as distinct from the earlier Etruscans). It remained a tribal organization until about 500BC when it became a republic and began to absorb the surrounding tribes, eventually extending its empire from Britain and France in the north, Spain in the west, Sicily, Carthage (modern Tunisia), Egypt and the eastern Mediterranean to the south; Greece and the Balkans to the east.

Architecturally, the golden age of Rome begins with the reign of Augustus (27BC– AD14) who boasted that when he came to power Rome was a city of brick but that he left it a city of marble. And it is true that before his reign little marble was used in Rome. From the 1st century AD the quarries of Carrara were developed and marble was imported from Hymettus and Pentelicus (which had supplied the marble for the

Colosseum, Rome, Italy, c. AD70.

Pantheon and plan, Rome, Italy, c.AD118–128.

Parthenon) in Greece.

Ancient Rome was a restless entrepreneurial-imperial society. It loved engineering because it made things in the empire work and thus made their conquests profitable, and it loved grandeur as the outward manifestation of its achievement. Rome's attitude to the Greeks was always ambiguous. One the one hand they despised the Greeks (because they were militarily and economically weak compared to Rome) but on the other were also in awe of their civilization. If the Romans had might the Greeks had style and class. Roman architects used the Greek Orders but added to them and would often use more than one on a building, something the Greeks would have dismissed as vulgar excess. Where Greek buildings rarely exceeded two stories built on the simple lintel, the Romans built up to four or five by using arches and vaults.

The Greeks used marble almost exclusively, but the Romans had access to a wide choice of materials: brick, marble, stone, tufa (a volcanic stone) and, most importantly, concrete which was crucially important in two of the greatest contributions Rome was to make to the history of architecture: the arch and the vault. During the years of the Republic (c.500–44BC) the Romans adopted the Greek timber-and-tiled roof, but during the Imperial era (27BC–AD337) when they needed great public buildings, like baths and basilicas, the roofs were often vaulted with brick and concrete which lent a rigidity that made possible such stupendous expanses like the great dome of the Pantheon in Rome (AD118–129).

Byzantine

The Roman Emperor Constantine moved his capital to Constantinople (ancient Byzantium, modern Istanbul) in AD 330 and established the Christian Roman Empire of the East. Christianity was now the official religion of the Empire so it is not surprising that churches, the most durably built and important structures in Byzantine society, are mainly what survive today.

The Byzantine Empire was strongly affected by three factors: Christianity, Hellenism (from the predominantly Greek population of Constantinople who provided most of the craftsmen) and the stylistic influence of the

S. Sophia, Istanbul, Turkey, AD532–37.

countries to the immediate east.

Byzantine architecture is the bridge between Roman and Romanesque, and one of its most distinctive characteristics was the dome. The Romans had their vaults but they could never fully develop the possibilities because the thrust forces could only be controlled if the dome was set on a circular base, as it was with the Pantheon. Byzantine builders broke out of these structural limitations by developing domes set on square walls. At first they used brackets (squinches) to create an octagonal base, but later refined this with pendentives (similar to supporting legs at each corner). This meant that huge domes could be built, the most famous being S. Sophia in Constantinople (AD532–7) built by Constantine's successor, Justinian (AD527–65), who had reunited the Eastern and Western Roman Empires and embarked on a breathtaking program of building: whole cities, aqueducts, fortifications, bridges, theaters, as well as many churches.

St Mark's, Venice, Italy, c.1040.

In addition to the great building projects of the 5th and 6th centuries, Byzantine architecture had a second flowering in the 11th century, and one of the greatest buildings of that second period is undoubtedly St Mark, Venice, a European city that had for centuries depended on trade with the east.

The influence of Byzantine architecture was widespread, particularly in Russia. The first great Byzantine church there was S. Sophia, Kiev in 1037 and the style flourished for many centuries. St Basil the Blessed in the Kremlin, Moscow, with its famous 'onion' domes is 16/17th century. Even as late as 1904 the Alexander Nevsky Cathedral, Sophia, Bulgaria, was built in full-blown Byzantine style.

Romanesque and Gothic: 10–15th centuries

The Church was the paramount authority throughout Europe, providing not only social and political stability but also intellectual and spiritual coherence. In the 11th and 12th centuries to build in granite, marble, or stone was an awesome undertaking, but with the Church's organizational, financial, and spiritual motivation vast buildings were undertaken throughout Europe. Although there are strong regional variations, the Romanesque style has some shared characteristics. It was based on simple, strong geometric forms with widespread use of the semicircular-headed arch; the use of the basilica form of church design; sturdy piers (often cylindrical) and thick walls; vaulting tended to be semicircular and often barrel-vaulted. Capitals were derived from Roman and Byzantine models, though simplified.

The prime movers of the Romanesque world were the monasteries, and in particular the Clunaic movement based at the Benedictine Abbey of Cluny in Burgundy, France. Although the Abbey was largely destroyed in 1810 its massive scale bore witness to the belief that God was owed the finest buildings Man could devise, not only in structural terms but also decoratively. Carving and wall painting were important

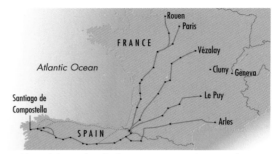

Map of the medieval pilgrimage routes to Santiago de Compostella, Spain.

elements in buildings designed to teach the Gospels to a largely illiterate congregation.

Religious relics attracted thousands of pilgrims from the length and breadth of Europe. The most famous destination was S. James church (begun 1077) at Santiago de Compostella in north-west Spain. Pilgrimage churches – often very sizable – are dotted all along the pilgrim routes of northern Spain, France, England, Germany, and Italy.

France is particularly rich in fine Romanesque churches. For example, S. Etienne, Caen, has a magnificent exterior of grouped masses and towers; Notre-Dame La Grande, Poitiers; Autun

Notre Dame La Grande, Poitiers, France, 11th and 12th centuries.

Cathedral and S. Madeleine, Vézelay, both in Burgundy; the Abbey of Fontevrault on the Loire; S. Foy, Conques, as well as S.Trophîme, Arles, are just a few of the more notable examples.

Romanesque architecture developed early in Germany and was at first much influenced by northern Italy due to the geo-political links between the two countries. Later, Germany developed its own Romanesque style: strongly dignified and austere. A characteristically German Romanesque feature was the church with an apse at each end: one for the abbot, the other for the bishop. Other German features were the dramatic towers, cupolas and turrets. In the Rhineland the greatest examples are Worms, Mainz, and Speyer cathedrals. A little further north is the magnificently preserved Abbey Church of Maria Laach (begun 1093) with its six towers and four apses. Further south on the Mosel is Trier cathedral and the Liebfrauenkirche, and in Bavaria the Schottenkirche at Regensburg.

In Italy, Sicily has a particularly rich Romanesque legacy. During this period the island was under Norman rule, but their northern style was mixed with Saracen and Byzantine influences: the cathedral of Monreale near Palermo is a good example of these entwined styles. Perhaps the most famous Italian buildings of this period are those of the Piazza dei Miracoli in Pisa, consisting of the Baptistery, Cathedral and, most famously, the Campanile (the 'Leaning Tower').

Pilgrimage church of S. Martín de Frómista, Spain, 1066.

In Spain there are fine Romanesque churches (in addition to S. James at Santiago de Compostella): Meira Abbey Church, the Abbey Church of S. Maria, Ripoll, and three in Segovia: S. Martín, S. Estéban, and S. Millán. One of the most classic of the pilgrimage churches of the north is S. Martín at Frómista. In the west, the most interesting examples are Zamora Cathedral, the Collegiate Church at Toro, the cathedral of Cuidad Rodrigo, and the Old Cathedral at Salamanca.

English Romanesque architecture is usually called 'Norman' after the dynasty founded in England by William I of Normandy in 1066. Norman building is found throughout the country, but undoubtedly the finest example is Durham cathedral (begun 1093), particularly the interior where its magnificent stone vaulting is a precursor of the Gothic. Other outstanding examples are the pilgrimage church of Southwell Minster (West front begun c.1130), and the keep ('White Tower') of the Tower of London (1078).

'Gothic' was first used as a term of disapproval, even contempt, by the Italian Renaissance historian and architect Giorgio Vasari (1511–74). In comparison with what he saw as his own enlightened age, he looked back to medieval architecture as backward, a product of the Dark Ages of the barbaric Goths, hence the name.

The exact start-date of any new movement is difficult to pin down exactly. Gothic evolved from the Romanesque but its spirit is very different. Where the Romanesque is solid and rooted to the earth, Gothic is light and soaring, and is defined by three architectural elements: the pointed arch, the ribbed vault, and the flying buttress, all of which are to be found in pre-Gothic buildings, but when combined define the Gothic style.

France, and particularly the Ile-de-France around Paris, was the cradle of the Gothic. No other country, and no single area within a country, can boast of such extraordinary architectural treasures. One of the first Gothic buildings was the great Abbey of S. Denis (started 1137), the life's work of the remarkable Abbé Suger. Born into a poor family in 1082 Suger was given as a child to the royal Abbey of S. Denis where he was educated with the king's son. In 1122 he became abbot and 15 years later was able to put into effect his long-cherished dream of rebuilding the abbey. Interestingly, Suger never made reference to the architecture of the

Notre Dame, Paris, France, begun 1163.

LEFT: Bourges Cathedral, France, begun 1190.
RIGHT: West front, Amiens Cathedral, France, 1220–88.

new building or commented on what was a new style; nor did he mention the name of the master-mason. S. Denis was soon followed by an astounding number of new cathedrals in the years between 1150 and 1300. Laon (1160–1225) whose west front was imitated throughout the 13th century at Chartres, Reims, Strasbourg, and Halberstadt. Notre Dame, Paris (1163–1330), with its triple west portal and magnificent flying buttresses; Bourges Cathedral (1190–1275) modeled on Notre Dame by Bishop Henry de Sully, brother of Bishop Eudes de Sully, who had built Notre Dame; Reims (begun 1211) perhaps the richest and most glorious, as would be expected from the Coronation Church of the Kings of France; Amiens (1220–88) a classic of the Ile-de-France pattern and an inspiration for Gothic cathedrals throughout Europe; Chartres, with its non-matching towers, fabulous windows (130, including the famous Rose Window) and exterior sculpture (2200 external figures), while Le Mans, further north, has 13 side chapels sprouting off the apse; Beauvais Cathedral in northern France is High Gothic (begun 1247) and designed on a vast scale. The choir (finished 1272) has the highest vaulted nave roof in Europe (157ft/52m) with a forest of flying buttresses as supports.

England developed its Gothic style early and clung to it much longer than any other European country. There were four phases. The first three – Transitional, Early English, and Decorated - followed developments in France, whereas the fourth, Perpendicular, was uniquely English and was to last from c.1375 to c.1560.

The outstanding example of Transitional is the choir of Canterbury Cathedral (1175-84); Early English is best represented by Salisbury Cathedral (1220–1258, the tower and spire a little later). Two fine examples of Decorated Gothic are the west fronts of Exeter and York cathedrals. The nave, south-west and central towers, cloisters, transepts, and Lady Chapel of Canterbury Cathedral illustrate Perpendicular at its best. Other examples are King's College Chapel, Cambridge (1446–1515); Eton College Chapel (1441), and St George's Chapel, Windsor (1475–1509).

Medieval Germany did not adopt the Gothic as readily as France or England. Until the end of the 13th century building was still in the Romanesque style. The earliest Gothic ecclesiastical building shows French influence, especially that of Amiens. A characteristic German feature was the twin- and single-towered west front. Cologne, begun 1248, and Regensburg, begun 1273, are examples of the twin-tower model, while the Minster of Ulm (begun 1377) is an outstanding example of the single-tower model.

The Hallenkirche, or hall church, was a

Cologne Cathedral and plan, begun 1248.

specifically German Gothic tradition where the vaults of the nave, choir, and aisles are all of the same height. One of the best examples of the Hallenkirche is the Marienkirche-zur-Wiese, Soest (started c.1340). The Hallenkirche style was influential in eastern Europe, particularly Poland, where there are a large number of brick examples (Church of the Assumption, Chelmno, the Collegiate Church of Our Lady, Poznan, and the Church of St John, Torun are among the finest).

The preeminent Gothic building in Czechoslovakia is S. Vitus Cathedral, Prague (begun by Matthieu of Arras in the 1340s in the French style, and finished by Peter Parler).

If the Gothic style is primarily a northern European phenomenon then it is not surprising that the outstanding example in Italy should appear either in the north of the country: Milan Cathedral (1387–1410) in Piedmont is the closest to northern Gothic and is covered with sculpture and pinnacles. Tuscany has some exceptional Gothic in the form of the cathedrals of Florence, Orvieto and, perhaps the greatest of the three, Siena (1245–1380) decorated in dramatic strips of black and white marble. Sicily has always been a crossroads of cultures as represented by the Cathedral of Palermo, (begun 1185), which is a mix of Norman and Moorish styles.

Doge's Palace, Venice, Italy, begun 1343.

Medieval Italy also produced a wealth of municipal building at this time. The most notable are the Palazzo Pubblico, Siena (1288–1309); the Palazzo Vecchio, Florence (1298–1344); Palazzo dei Priori, Volterra (13th century), and the Doge's Palace, Venice (1343–1438).

In Spain most of the Gothic work is in the north and dates mainly from the 13th century: Léon Cathedral is based on the French Ile-de-France type; Toledo Cathedral (begun 1226), one of the finest Gothic monuments in Europe; Burgos Cathedral (begun 1221) with its later German-style traceried spires (1486), and

Burgos Cathedral, Spain, begun 1221.

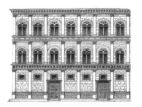 

Barcelona Cathedral (begun 1298 but completed by the 15th century). Late Gothic work is represented spectacularly by Seville Cathedral, the largest in Europe, which was built over a long period beginning in 1402 at the west end but not finished until c.1520.

Renaissance and Mannerism c.1420–1650

In Italian it is *Rinascimento*, in Spanish *Renacimento* while in England and Holland it is the French *Renaissance*. The words differ but the meaning is the same: rebirth.

The root of the Renaissance is found in the intellectual challenge to the Christian orthodoxy that had dominated Europe since the 4th century. Renaissance scholars of the 14th century, inspired by the traditions of Ancient Greece and Rome, promoted the idea of man as an individual human being, important in his own right: man as the measure of all temporal things. It is a reflection of this view that Renaissance buildings are discussed in terms of their architects whereas previously the architect had been almost universally anonymous. With the Renaissance the artist, whatever his medium, became an important member of society. That this Humanist philosophy should have been born in Italy is not surprising, for it had been the center of the Roman Empire, which itself had looked to Greece for inspiration.

The discovery of the manuscripts of the 1st century BC architect and engineer Vitruvius (Marcus Vitruvius Pollio) in 1414 inspired the pure Classicism of the High Renaissance (Classical is the adjective describing attributes of Ancient Greece and Rome; Classicism is the noun. Classic refers to styles that reflect some of the characteristics of an original style, whether its Classical, Romanesque, Byzantine etc). His books were translated into many languages and certain architects and schools of architecture relied heavily on them. Because they were now available in book form they could travel fast and wide in a way that was impossible in the oral tradition of the Middle Ages.

Filippo Brunelleschi (1377–1446) is generally considered to be the first Renaissance architect.

His early work, like the Ospedale degli Innocenti (Foundlings Hospital), Florence (begun 1419), shows a new Classical approach with careful proportioning of parts and an overall sense of symmetry. In 1420 he brought all his mathematical skills and the knowledge he had gained from studying ancient Roman vaults to solve the problem of how to create a dome for the medieval Florence Cathedral. It stands as one of the great engineering feats of the Renaissance.

Pazzi chapel, S. Croce, Florence, Italy, 1429–61, by Brunelleschi.

Leone Battista Alberti (1404–72) was chiefly responsible for formulating Renaissance architectural theory in his *Ten Books on Architecture*, itself based on the work of Vitruvius. Alberti's pioneering study helped to establish the status of architecture as an art, rather than a mere trade, as it had been viewed previously. He was a great disseminator of Classical forms who

LEFT: *Santa Maria Novella, Florence, Italy, 1470, by Alberti.*
RIGHT: *Palazzo Rucellai, Florence, Italy, begun 1453, by Alberti.*

took Renaissance architecture from Florence to the rest of Italy, undertaking buildings in Rimini and Mantua. He was also instrumental in persuading Pope Julius II to undertake a complete reconstruction of the ancient Basilica of St Peter in Rome, which became the greatest architectural undertaking of the Renaissance.

The 16th century, the Cinquecento, was the great age of the Renaissance in Italy. Among the wealth of artists three stand above the others: Bramante, Raphael, and Michelangelo. Donato d'Agnolo Lazzari, known as Bramante (1444–1514), came from Urbino and made his reputation in Milan as a strict Classicist. He went to Rome and established himself as the leading architect of the day and, like Brunelleschi, was attracted to the symmetry of the circular church. He experimented with the form in his little temple, Il Tempietto (1502–10), erected in the courtyard of S. Pietro in Montorio, Rome. In 1505 it was to Bramante that Pope Julius turned to for the new design for St Peter's and, in essence,

Il Tempietto, S. Pietro in Montorio, Rome, Italy, 1500–10, by Bramante.

Bramante's design is an elaboration of his work on Il Tempietto. Work started on St Peter's according to Bramante's plan, but his death in 1514 put the project on hold until Michelangelo took it up in 1547.

Michelangelo Buonarroti (1475–1564). His work in Florence, particularly the Medici Mausoleum (1519–34), and the Biblioteca Laurenziana (1524–71), with their distortions of the strictly Classical, began the move to Mannerism, a transitional Renaissance style between High Renaissance and the Baroque. In 1547 Michelangelo began what he saw as his greatest work, St Peter's, Rome, on which he spent the last two decades of his life, refusing any payment. He abandoned Bramante's circular

St Peter's Rome, Italy, with Bramante's plan of 1506 and Michelangelo's plan of 1547.

plan for St Peter's in favor of a Latin cross, and although the basilica is much changed from Michelangelo's original concept, his is still the single greatest contribution. Michelangelo was also interested in large scale civic works, mostly spectacularly represented by his complete remodeling of the Piazza del Campidoglio (Capitol Hill), Rome (begun in 1540) where he changed a jumble of buildings on a hill into an orderly square approached by a majestic flight of steps.

If Michelangelo had signaled Mannerism other architects of the later 16th century developed it more fully. The most influential was Giulio Romano (1499–1546), a pupil of Raphael, and the creator of the highly idiosyncratic Palazzo del Te (1525–32), Mantua, where novel decorative effect takes precedence over structural necessity. Sebastiano Serlio (1475–1554) is important for his impact (mainly through his treatises) on the Renaissance in France, particularly at Fontainebleau which was the center of French Mannerism.

Andrea Palladio (1508–80) was the greatest

Villa Capra, Vicenza, Italy, begun c.1550, by Palladio.

architect of the second half of the 16th century, and his strict adherence to Classical Antiquity and the works of Vitruvius is the opposite of the indulgences of the Mannerists. He worked on domestic villas as well as churches in and around Venice. As influential as his buildings were his treatises, *The Four Books of Architecture* and *The Antiquities of Rome* which were translated into many languages and had a profound impact on architects in France, England, Germany, and America. Two outstanding examples of his work are the Palazzo Chierricati (1550 but not completed until late in the 17th century) at Vicenza, and the Villa Capra (also known as the La Rotonda, c.1550–69) outside Vicenza, which was to have a particularly powerful appeal to English Palladians of the 18th century. Two of his greatest churches are to be found within Venice itself: S. Giorgio Maggiore (1565) and Il Redentore (1577–92).

France was the first European country outside Italy to adopt Renaissance forms, but it was not until the later part of the 16th century that native French architects began to build in the style. King François I was a pioneer patron of architecture, first at the Château of Blois and then at the Château of Chambord (begun 1519).

Cour des Adieux, Fontainebleau, France, 1528–40, by Gilles de Breton.

Azay-le-Rideau, France, 1518–29.

Ayuntamiento (town hall), Seville, Spain, begun 1534, by Diego de Riaño.

In 1528 he decided to enlarge the medieval castle at Fontainebleau and entrusted Gilles le Breton with the task. The work was to have a decisive affect and encourage French architects to develop their own Renaissance style. One was Philibert de l'Orme (c.1510–70), a descendant of a long line of master-masons who, with Jean Bullant (c.1520–78), built the new Tuileries Palace in Paris (destroyed 1871). Pierre Lescot (c.1510 or 1515–1578) is most famous for his work at the Louvre, again an initiative of François I, where Lescot created, for the first time in France, facades based on Italian lines.

In England Henry VIII encouraged Italian craftsmen, but his break with the Church of Rome delayed the introduction of Renaissance architectural styles. More influential in England was Flemish Mannerism with its emphasis on surface decoration. The great houses of the period (there was not much ecclesiastical building) are a lively mixture of Elizabethan structures and Renaissance decoration. Prominent examples are Longleat (1550–80), Hardwick Hall (1591–7), Montacute (1588–1601), and Wollaton Hall (1580–5). It was Inigo Jones (1573–1652), the first truly professional architect in England, who brought the Italian Renaissance to England after having traveled in Italy where he was greatly influenced by Palladio. His outstanding buildings are the Queen's House (1616–22), Greenwich, and the Banqueting Hall (1619–22), Whitehall, London.

On the Iberian peninsula there were three

The Queen's House, Greenwich, England, 1616–35, by Inigo Jones.

stages of Renaissance architecture. The first, Renaissance Plateresque (the word comes from the decoration on silver plate), saw the application of surface decoration to what were still medieval-style buildings (the facade of Salamanca University, 1516–29, and the Palacio Municipal at Baeza in southern Spain, 1559 are notable). The second stage retained the rich decoration of the Plateresque but moved towards

Renaissance construction (examples are the Ayuntamiento [town hall], Seville [1534–72]; Luna Palace [now the Audiencia], Zaragosa, 1537–52, and the University of Alcalà de Henares near Madrid, c.1550). The third stage was of a much purer Classical expression and mainly built in the late 16th and early 17th centuries. The architect most responsible for establishing this style was Juan de Herrera (c.1530–97) who had studied in Italy. His most famous work is the Escorial palace (1559–84) outside Madrid, a building of awesome severity. Juan Gómez de Mora (1586–1647) followed in Herrera's tradition. His finest achievement is the Plaza Mayor, Madrid,1617–20 (though initially planned by Herrera).

The Netherlands resisted full-blown Classicism until the end the 16th century and tended to use Renaissance motifs primarily as decorative elements on medieval buildings – a style known as Flemish Mannerism which was very influential in England. The outstanding 16th example is the Town Hall, Antwerp (1561–5) by Cornelius Floris (1514–75). As with England, a purer classical style did not emerge until the 17th century. Lieven de Key (1560–1627) and Hendrik de Keyser (1565–1621) were the leading architects of their day. De Key designed the Leyden Town Hall (1597) and the Butchers' Guild Hall, Haarlem (1602). De Keyser is best represented by the Amsterdam Exchange (1605), Delft Town Hall (1618) as well as three churches in Amsterdam: Zuiderkerk, Westkerk, and the Noorderkerk. The beginning of pure Renaissance Classicism came in the second quarter of the 17th century with the advent of Dutch Palladianism, the chief example of which is the Mauritshuis at the Hague (1633) designed by Pieter Post (1608–69) and Jacob van Campen (1595–1657).

In Germany too it was not until the 17th century that a true Renaissance style became established. The finest example is Elias Holl's (1573–1646) Augsburg Town Hall (1615–20). Holl had traveled to Italy and was a particular admirer of Palladio and Sansovino.

Baroque and Rococo, 17th & 18th centuries

The word Baroque derives from the Portuguese *barroco* (Spanish *barrueco*) and, like Gothic, was originally a derogatory term referring to what was seen as the bizarre, sometimes bulbous, curves that characterized the style.

The Baroque originated in Italy, more specifically Rome, as an expression of the religious fervor associated with the Catholic Counter-Reformation, and it was in other European Catholic countries that it had most impact, particularly Spain, Portugal (and through them their South American colonial possessions), Bavaria, Austria, and France.

Its main characteristics were the free use of curves within a classical framework; the use of dramatic lighting effects, and the combination of painting and sculpture to create the 'theater'

of the architectural experience, often using trompe l'oeil ('cheating the eye') painting techniques. At its best the Baroque is rich, sensuous and dramatic; at its worst, insufferably hysterical.

Two of the greatest exponents were Gianlorenzo Bernini (1598–1680), and Francesco Borromini (1599–1667). Both were painters, architects and poets, but considered sculpture as their true calling. In 1629 Bernini became architect of St Peter's, Rome, and designed the baldacchino (canopy) over the high altar. He also built the great embracing double-curve arms of the colonnade on the piazza in front of St Peter's. In 1645 he designed the sensationally theatrical Cornaro Chapel in Santa Maria della Vittoria, Rome, and between 1648 and 1651 laid out the Piazza Navona, Rome, a masterpiece of planning.

S. Agnese, begun 1652, Piazza Navona, Rome, Italy, by Rainaldi and Borromini.

His finest work is Sant'Andrea al Quirinale (1658-70) which was to have a great impact on Baroque church building in central Europe.

Borromini went much further than Bernini in challenging classical norms. S. Carlo alle Quattro Fontane (1638–40) was his first church and it caused a sensation. He went on to remodel S. John Lateran and created a fine Baroque exterior for S. Agnese in the Piazza Navona (1652–6). His use of opposing curves was an important influence on the exuberant Rococo of southern Germany and Austria.

The last great buildings of Venice were also influenced by the Baroque. A good example is the Salute church, Venice (1632) by Baldassare Longhena (1598–1682) with its dome seemingly supported on elaborate scrolls. The dome for the Chapel of the Holy Shroud, Turin, by Guarino Guarini (1624–83) deserves its place among Baroque masterworks.

France produced some exceptional Baroque architecture, if more tempered and less excitable than its Italian neighbor. The chief architect of the early 17th century was Salomon de Brosse (1571–1626) whose preeminent work is the Palais de Luxembourg (started 1614) built for Marie de' Medici, wife of Louis XIII. The middle years of the 17th century saw the rise of a

The garden front, Château Vaux-le-Vicomte, France, by Louis Le Vau.

number of great French architects: Jacques Lemercier, c.1585–1654 (Church of the Sorbonne, Paris, and the church of the University of Paris); François Mansart, 1598–1666 (the Baroque central block of the Château de Blois, the church of Val de Grâce, Paris, completed by Lemercier); Louis Le Vau, 1612–70 (Institut de France in refined Baroque, Château de Vaux-le-Vicomte, and substantial parts of Versailles). Jules Hardouin Mansart ,1646–1708 (church of S. Louis des Invalides; the Place Vendôme and Place des Victoires, as well as extensive work at Versailles, particularly the royal chapel, stables, orangery, and Grand Trianon)

In England the outstanding architect of this period, and perhaps the greatest of any period of English history, was Sir Christopher Wren (1632–1723). His most famous work is, of course,

St Paul's Cathedral and plan, begun 1675, London, England, by Sir Christopher Wren.

St Paul's Cathedral, London (1675–1710) with its restrained Baroque features. He was also responsible for a large number of London churches (St Bride's Fleet Street, 1680–1701; St Stephen Walbrook, 1675–87; and St Lawrence Jewry, 1670-86, are outstanding examples). Wren's finest secular works are the Royal Hospital, Greenwich (completed 1752), a "palace of Baroque monumentality", and the Royal Hospital, Chelsea (1682–92). Other significant architects of the time were Sir John Vanbrugh (1664–1726) and Nicholas Hawksmoor (1661–1736). Vanbrugh, playwright, soldier and wit (though, like many, not a formally trained architect), designed Castle Howard, Yorkshire (1699–1712). At Blenheim Palace (1705–22) Vanbrugh was allowed full rein and the huge edifice stands as the pinnacle of English Baroque. Hawksmoor had worked with Wren on many of his greatest projects and assisted Vanbrugh on Castle Howard and Blenheim. He is best remembered for six highly original churches in London, of which Christ Church, Spitalfields (1714–29) is probably the finest.

Germany had suffered terribly during the Thirty Years War (1618–48) and Austria was under pressure from invading Turks until the 1680s. As a consequence, the Baroque did not fully develop in these countries until about 1700, but once it did there was a flowering of some of the greatest Baroque building in Europe. At first it was architects of Italian origin – Barelli, Zuccali, Viscardi – who worked in Italian Baroque forms (typical examples are the Cathedral of Passau and the Theatinerkirche, Munich). Of Austro-German architects the outstanding practitioners were: Daniel Pöppelman (1662–1736) in Dresden (The Zwinger,1711–20); Balthasar Neumann (1687–1753) in Würzburg (the Residenz, 1719–53 in collaboration with the painter Tiepolo and, perhaps his masterpiece, the

Vierzehnheiligen Pilgrimage Church, Franconia of 1743-62); the Austrian Johann Bernard Fischer von Erlach (1656–1723) in Vienna (Karlskirche, 1716; the Palace of Schönbrunn – the Versailles of Austria; National Library begun

The Zwinger, Dresden, Germany, 1711–20, by Daniel Pöppelman.

1722; Imperial Chancellery wing of the Hofburg, 1729); Lucas von Hilderbrandt (1668–1745) in Vienna (Upper Beleverdere, 1721–23); and Jacob Prandtauer (1660–1726) whose chief building was the remodeling of the great Abbey of Melk on the river Danube in 1702.

In Spain and Portugal, following the austerity of the early Renaissance, Baroque was adopted with a passion. One of the greatest monuments to Spanish Baroque is the Transparente in Toledo Cathedral (1721-32) by Narciso Tomé (c.1694–1742), which has been described as a "fricassee of marble." But even this was mild compared to the work of José de Churriguera (1650–1725) and his family and followers (Pedro de Ribera's Hospicio San Fernando, Madrid, begun 1722, and Francisco Izquierdo's sacristy in the Cartuja, Grenada, 1713, are good examples of Churrigueresque, as the high-octane decorative style was called).

Rococo (from the French *rocaille* or seashell) was a lighter and more playful extension of the Baroque rather than a full-blown style in its own right. It originated in France and was taken up enthusiastically in Germany, Austria and Russia, but had little impact in Protestant Europe or America. The French architect François Cuvilliés (1695-1768) was one of the leading architects in the Rococo idiom, especially in Bavaria where he was Court architect. His Amalienburg hunting lodge of the Nymphenburg Palace, Munich (1734–9) is a Rococo jewel.

Neoclassicism c.1750-c.1830

The return to strict Classical forms in European and American architecture involved many factors, but foremost was the realization that Baroque and Rococo had only one way to go – towards greater and greater elaboration - until its inevitable expiration in a swirl of clouds and cherubim. The mid-18th century witnessed the emergence of archaeology and with it a renewed interest in the ancient civilizations of Egypt, Greece, and Rome, the birthplaces of the Classical (Napoleon's campaigns in Egypt also stimulated a huge passion for things *Egyptienne*). In an age of absolute monarchies the Classical order seemed a suitable outward expression of control, something the French Revolution briefly interrupted but which Napoleon strongly reasserted. In France we can see such examples as the Ste-Geneviève, Paris (1756, renamed the Panthéon) by Jacques-Germain Soufflot (1713–80); and the Temple de la Gloire, Paris (1806, renamed the Madeleine in 1813) by Alexandre-Pierre Vignon (1762–1828).

In England the Palladian movement also championed Classical principles. Leading proponents were patron and architect Lord

The Panthéon, Paris, France, 1756, by Jacques-Germain Soufflot.

Burlington (1694–1753) whose Chiswick House, 1723-9, has been called the "manifesto of English Palladians"; William Kent (1685–1748) represented by Holkham Hall (begun 1734); Robert Adam (1728–92) by Kenwood House (1767-8) and Syon House (1761-70); and the remodeling of Regent's Park and other parts of

Chiswick House, England, 1725, by Lord Burlington.

central London by John Nash (1752–1835).

Some of the most outstanding Neo-Classical works of the early 19th century were to be found in Germany: the Glyptothek, Munich (1815–34) by Leo von Klenze (1784–1864), and perhaps the greatest of all Karl Friedrich Schinkel (1781–1841) who, apart from being the architect of genius of his age, was also a painter, stage-

The Glypothek, Munich, Germany, begun 1815, by Leo von Klenze.

designer, intellectual, and gifted draughtsman, his Neue Wache (New Guard House, Berlin 1816–18), the Schauspielhaus (1819-21), and the Altes Museum, his masterwork (1823–30) were later purchased by the Prussian state as national treasures.

NORTH AMERICA: As might be expected Colonial America took its architectural lead from England. On the Eastern Seaboard the buildings had the simple integrity of the Puritan founders, while in Virginia, where the English settlers had come from more aristocratic origins, the principal buildings tended to be more grandiose. Both, however, reflected the influence of their colonial overlord, with the town of Williamsburg (though now much restored) as the single greatest monument of the Colonial era. It was not until the 18th century that named American (though often English-born) architects began to appear, people like Peter Harrison (1716–75) the builder of King's Chapel, Boston (1749) among others. Thomas Jefferson (1743–1826) was not only one

Mount Vernon, Virginia, USA, 1774-86, by George Washington.

LEFT: Traditional meets the Modern: The Plaza Hotel, 1907, by Henry J. Hardenbergh and 9 West 57th Street, New York, USA, 1972, by Skidmore, Owings & Merrill.
Right: Palace of Westminster, London, England, begun 1834, by Sir Charles Barry and A.W.N. Pugin.

Reading Room, Bibliothèque Nationale, Paris, France, begun 1854, by Henri Labrouste.

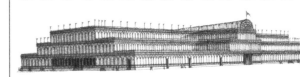

The Crystal Palace, London, England, 1851, by Sir Joseph Paxton.

of the co-authors of the Declaration of Independence and the third President of the fledgling republic but also a superb Classically-inspired architect, as attested by his own home at Monticello (begun 1769), the State Capitol of Virginia (1785–99), and the University of Virginia (1817–26). Charles Bullfinch (1763–1844) was also an architect inspired by the Classical (Massachusetts State House, 1793–1800), as was another English-born architect Benjamin Henry Latrobe (1764–1820), the first Surveyor of Public Buildings in the USA, who had advised Jefferson on University of Virginia and worked on the Capitol, Washington, DC. His finest building is probably the Roman Catholic Cathedral of Baltimore (1804–18).

Virginia State Capitol, USA, center building, 1785–92 by Thomas Jefferson (wings added 1904–6).

The Birth of the Modern

Towards the end of the 18th century two political revolutions – the American and the French – as well as the onset of the Industrial Revolution, set in motion forces that would transform our world to an extent unprecedented in recorded history. Now, at the beginning of the 21st century we are so conscious of the enormous changes of the past few decades that it is sometimes difficult to accept that these earlier revolutions were far greater yet. For the first time in history communications were not limited to the speed of a horse or a wind-driven sailing vessel. Steam-powered machinery revolutionized transportation, communications and manufacturing, and by the 1830s the transformation of Western societies from static to dynamic was well underway. For example, nails used in building construction were no longer forged by hand but produced by machines a hundred times faster. Wrought iron became available for structural use in buildings, and by the 1880s steel made possible the structural cage – skeleton construction – that freed walls from their traditional task of supporting floors and roofs.

In response to these enormous changes it would have been only natural to see the emergence of a new and revolutionary kind of architecture. What happened instead was a retreat into eclecticism: the copying of the outward forms of past historical styles so that by the mid-nineteenth century it appeared as if an architect's first decision on a project was whether to imitate Gothic or Classical forms.

While Gothic eclecticism had some forceful advocates (notably A.W.N. Pugin, 1812–52, in England) it was Classical eclecticism that became the dominant architectural style. All over the world, irrespective of the building's function, the local climate, or any other considerations, many public buildings were sheathed in the quasi-respectability of classical forms.

Modern architecture came into being as a reaction against this retrograde nostalgia. It sought to create a new architectural language that reflected the changing needs of society and of the materials and building technologies that had become available. As it evolved it became increasingly concerned with responding to local climate, materials, and the characteristics of the site itself.

In the centuries-old traditional way of building (which culminated in the 1820s) technology had remained essentially unchanged. The load-bearing envelope was the defining characteristic of the structure, and the hand of the craftsman shaped everything. This is what had given buildings their authenticity and integrity. To a large extent the movement that gave birth to modern architecture was driven by a need to recapture that quality of genuineness. Modern architecture, so often thought in terms of an avant-garde rejection of tradition, in fact strove to return to a focus on functionalism. In fact, modern architecture should be seen as an effort to recapture the traditional values that had given buildings their authenticity. (It is interesting that the title of Le Corbusier's most famous book, *Vers une Architecture (Towards an Architecture)* was not, as an early translator called it, *Towards a New Architecture*). The primary goal of the modern movement was to return to basic principles rather than blindly copying external forms. No wonder that Mies van der Rohe's favorite quotation was drawn from St Augustine: "Beauty is the radiance of truth."

All these precepts are found in the writings of the intellectual father of modern architecture, the French architect and theoretician Eugène-Emanuel Viollet-le-Duc (1814–79). Most of his professional career was dedicated to the restoration of some of the greatest of the Gothic buildings (Notre Dame and Sainte Chapelle in Paris, for example). In his writings (the *Lectures on Architecture* [1860], and the *Dictionnaire Raisonné de l'Architecture*, 1854–68) he advocated a structural rationalism that would provide the foundation for a new kind of architecture that was responsive to "the nature of the materials employed, to the climate, to the customs of an era, and to the necessities of the moment." Those architects and theorists who

followed in the 20th century would mostly do no more than elaborate on Viollet-le-Duc's ideas.

One of the earliest exponents of this new architecture was another Frenchman, Henri Labrouste (1801–75), with his Bibliothèque Ste-Geneviève (1830–50), and the reading room and book stacks of the Librairie Nationale (1854–75). Perhaps even more prophetic was the prefabricated iron-and-glass Crystal Palace built for the 1851 Great Exhibition in London from a design by Sir Joseph Paxton (1803–65). However, in an age of great engineering feats, it was the bridges, railroad sheds, factory and mill buildings that proved to be the most influential of all.

Modern architecture can be said to have been born in Chicago in the 1880s. The steel skeleton structure was first used by William LeBaron Jenney (1832–1907) in the Home Insurance Building, Chicago, in 1884. Three architectural firms: Adler and Sullivan, Burnham and Root, and Holabird and Roche, played a major role in shaping an architectural language for this totally new building type. The towering figure among them was Louis H. Sullivan (1856–1924) who proclaimed that a skyscraper should be a "proud and soaring thing" and proceeded to demonstrate how it could be done in a succession of increasingly articulated and expressive office towers culminating in the Guaranty (also known as the Prudential) Building (1895) in Buffalo, New York. Then, following the dissolution of his partnership with Adler, he demonstrated how the steel structural cage should be expressed in the Carson, Pirie, Scott store building (1899–1904) in Chicago.

Sullivan's disciple, Frank Lloyd Wright

LEFT: The Guaranty Building, Buffalo, New York, USA, 1895, by Louis Sullivan.
RIGHT: Bayard (originally Condict) Building, New York, USA, 1898, by Louis Sullivan.

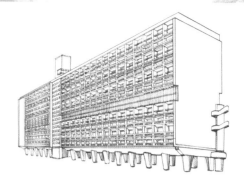

L'Unité d'Habitation, Marseilles, France, 1946–52, by Le Corbusier.

(1869–1959), showed that space in a building could be flowing and dynamic rather than compartmentalized and static. After Wright, the two most influential architects of the 20th century were Mies van der Rohe (1886–1959) and Le Corbusier (1887–1965), both of whom created seminal works in the 1920s and achieved a position of preeminence after World War II. By then modern architecture had emerged from its heroic period of struggle and achieved acceptance and recognition.

The generation of Mies van der Rohe and Le

LEFT: Solomon R. Guggenheim Museum, New York, USA, 1959, by Frank Lloyd Wright.
RIGHT: National Gallery, Berlin, Germany, 1962–8, by Mies van der Rohe.

Salk Institute, La Jolla, California, USA, 1959-65, by Louis Kahn.

Corbusier, as well as Walter Gropius (1883–1969) and Alvar Aalto (1898–1976), was succeeded by a new generation of architects, including among many others, Eero Saarinen (1910–61), Louis Kahn (1901–74), Oscar Niemeyer (b.1907), and Arne Jacobsen (1902–71). In fact, so overwhelming was the new modernist orthodoxy that it embraced the great majority of architects. No longer was it the province of an elite group of idealistic, deeply committed individuals. Now it was practiced by almost everyone – from the very good to the utterly derivative – which, in its turn, lead to a counter-movement,

Lever House, New York, USA, 1952, by Skidmore, Owings & Merrill.

Postmodernism, spearheaded by Robert Venturi's Complexity and *Contradiction in Architecture* (1966) and Philip Johnson's AT&T Building (1978) in New York City. But modern architecture, still rooted in the principles of structural rationalism, clarity, and integrity as well as the concerns of sustainability, is still alive and thriving in the work of such architects as Richard Rogers, Norman Foster, I.M. Pei, Renzo Piano and many others.

China

DYNASTY TIMELINE

206BC – AD220	Han
265–420	Chin
581–618	Sui
618–907	T'ang
960–1279	Sung
1279–1368	Yüan
1368–1644	Ming
1644–1911	Ch'ing

Compared to Europe there are not as many old buildings in China. In fact, there is hardly anything remaining before the Ming dynasty. Unlike Europe there was not an emphasis on innovation; buildings tended to be rebuilt or refurbished in traditional styles throughout Chinese history. It was a highly conservative tradition with only subtle changes of style across the centuries. Although masonry was used (the arch and vault were known early in Chinese history), it was employed mainly for fortifications, bridges, and engineering works. The primary material was wood which, although allowing great flexibility, was also prone to decay.

It may seem odd to speak about common architectural principles that span 2,000 years, but the basic uniformity and standardization of the Chinese tradition unites all, both in structure and planning. The most striking is the reliance on timber for the frame construction common to Chinese buildings.

What are considered 'typical' Chinese architectural features appeared during the 4th-6th centuries: overhanging eaves, curved roof line, bracket clusters, and columns spaced at intervals rather than walls. And it was during the Han dynasty that the characteristic ground plan was developed and remained stable through the centuries. The building complex was surrounded by a protective wall (privacy was highly valued). The typical home was set within a walled enclosure around a courtyard with the principal rooms oriented on a north-south axis. The east and west buildings were lower, and in one of these the servants would have been housed. Heating was from a portable charcoal brazier, although the Chinese preferred to dress more warmly during winter rather than rely on external heating. The kitchen was rarely an integral part of the building and was usually out in the open air in a verandah or outhouse.

The role of the architect was very different to

P'ai lou to the Ming tombs, Beijing, China, 1522–66.

the post-Renaissance European conception. Building techniques and designs were passed down in an oral tradition and rigidly limited by custom and convention. Sumptuary laws laid down what kind of building was suitable for different grades and distinctions of social class. A client 'ordered' a building like any other commodity, and the different types and construction and their suitability for different uses were so well known that the design was a foregone conclusion. Architecture in China tended to be created collectively, fed by slow-moving traditions and less by the 'vision' of an individual.

The 'Enemy Observation Pagoda', Hopei, China, c.1055.

China was largely a secular country and, unlike Hindu India, Christian Europe, or the Islamic world, not dominated by one over-arching theology. Confucianism was more a socio-political doctrine, and Taoism was less a religion and more a philosophy. Buddhism arrived from India to China in the 1st century AD but its buildings tended to be constructed within the Chinese secular tradition, with walled enclosures and hall styles. However, Buddhism did contribute some unique architectural forms: the pagoda (based on the Indian stupa), the p'ai-lou or

Pagoda of the Sung Yüeh temple, Honan, China, AD523.

The Great Wall, China, c.221BC and 15th–16th centuries.

ceremonial arch (the most famous being five-arched example at the Ming tombs near Beijing, 1522–66), and the rock-cut temple and shrine (the Cave of the Thousand Buddhas at Tun-huang, begun AD366 and the 11th century Mai-chi Shan, T'ien-shui, Kansu province, span the tradition).

Above: The Forbidden City, Beijing, China, 15th century.

Fine examples of the pagoda are, in date order: Sung Yüeh, Honan province (AD523) which is the oldest surviving brick building in China; the 'Big Goose Pagoda' (AD652) of the Tz'u-en monastery in Sian, one of the few surviving buildings of the T'ang dynasty's great capital at Ch'ang-an, and the sung dynasty 'Enemy Observation Pagoda' at the K'ai Yüan temple in Ting-hsien (completed 1055), built of stone.

Temple of Heaven, Forbidden City, Beijing, China, 15th century.

Most of the few timber buildings that survive before the Ming dynasty are Buddhist temple halls. From the T'ang dynasty there is the Fo-kuang temple (AD857), Shansi province is the earliest wooden building in China. Another fine example is the Kuan-yin hall of the Tu-lo temple in the walled city of Chi-hsian, Hopei province, AD984.

THE GREAT WALL. Built by the engineer Ch'in Shih Huang-ti (221–210BC) the Great Wall was in fact a joining together of walls already built by previous feudal states. Nevertheless it was a colossal undertaking only made possible by conscripted labor. The total length is 2,484 miles/828km, originally of rammed earth. It was in the 15th and 16th centuries under the Ming that the most extensive repairs and refacing with stone and brick took place.

IMPERIAL PEKING (BEIJING). 'Pei-ching' the 'Northern Capital' had existed since about 2400BC when there was a Neolithic settlement. Between AD1153–1215 it was the capital of the kingdom of the 'Golden Tartars', and from 1215–1368 of the Mongols. In 1403 the Ming dynasty moved its capital to Peking from Nanking and the city has remained architecturally stable since then. It has four main parts: the Outer City to the south, the Inner City to the north, and the Imperial City (within the Inner) that contains the Forbidden City. Compared to European cities it is large and the whole complex was planned as a unity. The emphasis is on grouped structures rather than individual buildings. Even the Throne Hall itself (T'ai-ho Tien), for all its size, is rich rather than dominating which reflects, perhaps, a less pretentious way of expressing the power and prestige of the monarch than would have been found in Renaissance Europe.

Japan

For much of its history Japan was isolated from outside influences, and those that did have an impact on its cultural, spiritual, and architectural traditions, primarily Korea, China, and Buddhist India, evolved slowly and continuously. The basic forms tended to be constant and changes relatively small. Timber was the main building material because it proved most resistant to the earthquakes to which Japan is prone. A side effect of its use has been the constant re-construction of old buildings in exact replication of the original, often as frequently as every 20 years. Climate has also had a fundamental role in Japanese building style. The characteristic overhang of the classic Japanese roof enables it to throw off the very heavy annual rainfall. To combat the high humidity of summer buildings were raised on open wooden platforms, and movable interior screens (wood or paper-covered frames called fusuma) allowed air to circulate throughout the building. As in China, the rigors of cold and dry winters were met with stoicism and extra layers of warm clothes.

PREHISTORY. The earliest architectural evidence comes from the Neolithic Jomon people who probably reached Japan from north and central Asia via Korea, and their pit-and-post huts (tateana) date from c. 1000BC. The Yayoi culture, originally of Asiatic or Oceanic derivation and centered on Kyushu, marked an advance in building techniques. Their dwellings (2nd–5th centuries AD) had pile-supported high floors entered by steps or a ladder, typical of Oceanic cultures. Some of the main monuments that survive are great funeral tumulii around the plain of Yamato, south-east of Osaka, which are probably inspired by the stupas of Buddhist India. It is also from this period that the traditional form of Shinto (a pantheistic nature-centered religion) shrines was established, the two greatest being the Ise Naiku and Ise Geku dating from the third quarter of the 5th century AD. With its emphasis on natural building materials and the relationship of buildings to nature, Shinto has had a continuously profound effect on Japanese architecture.

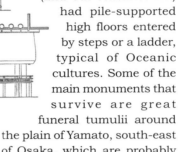
Ise Naiku shrine, Japan, 5th century AD.

ASUKA PERIOD (AD538–645). The imperial clan became established, with close ties to both Korea and northern China, and it was from Korea that Buddhism was introduced in 538 which, by the end of the 6th century, had been embraced by the Imperial house. Under imperial patronage were founded the great Buddhist temples of

Horyu-ji, Japan, AD 607.

Haiyu-ji, Hokyi, Hamji, and Horyu-ji , built 607, with the pagoda, gatehouse, and kondo (main sanctuary) surviving.

NARA PERIOD (645–793). In the 7th century direct relations were established with the Chinese T'ang Dynasty at its capital Ch'ang-an, which was closely copied in the new capital of Nara in 710. Some of the buildings that survive from this period are the temple-monasteries of the Todai-ji (founded 745) and the Toshodai-ji which, despite much rebuilding, still retain enough original structures to illustrate their style and scale: elaborate roofs of glazed tile, columns painted in vermilion, overhanging eaves and glorious painted decoration, the low Buddha hall, and the pagodas that had superseded the older stupa style. The Todai-ji was the largest monastery in Japan, far bigger than anything even in China. The Daibutsuden, or Hall of the Great Buddha, of the Todai-ji is the largest wooden building under one roof in the world and contains the largest bronze statue in the world.

Todai-ji, Japan, founded 745.

HEIAN PERIOD (794–1185). As was the custom when an emperor died the capital city was moved, in this case from Nara to Heian-Kyo (now Kyoto) and again the new city was laid out along Chinese lines. It was also in this period that two Buddhist sects were introduced to Japan, Shingon and Tendai, and with them a mass of minor Buddhist divinities that needed to be housed in ever more elaborate shrines and temples. By 898, however, the nobility showed a greater hostility towards foreign ideas and, in opposition to Shingon and Tendai, favored the

A Shinden dwelling, Japan.

cult of Amida (Jodo) which embraced anyone who worshipped the Buddha. Many temples were built by emperors and nobility, and of those that survive the pagoda of Daigoji, the Sangen-in, and the lecture halls of the Koryu-ji and Horyu-ji monasteries are most notable. The palaces of the nobility also became more elaborate in the shinden-zukuri style (where interconnected rectangular buildings were set in an intricate series of naturalistic gardens and waterways) that is regarded as one of the typical features of Japanese architecture.

KAMAKURA PERIOD (1185–1337). The ascendancy of the Minamoto clan brought with it a military-style government of the samurai at Kamakura, just south of Tokyo. The Zen sect of Buddhism, with its emphasis on self-discipline and simplicity, had a particular appeal to the warrior caste who now sought to cleanse the temples of their multi-deity statues and concentrate on the Buddha figure alone. In their domestic building, too, they created a more unified layout of rooms grouped under one roof with public spaces

The essential elements of the Islamic mosque were established by Muhammad's own very simple houses in Medina: the *qibla* wall facing in the direction of Mecca, and within this wall the *mihrab*.

By 750 the Umayyads had been defeated by the Abbasids (who were to hold power until 950) and the center of power moved to Baghdad in 762 under Caliph Al Mansur. Although no trace of Mansur's Baghdad survives, the great fortress-palace of Ukhaidar (780) remains. Samarra, Iraq, was founded in 836 and its remaining buildings show the origins of the four-centered arch, and the first domed tomb, both precedents of the rich tradition of Islamic architecture that followed. The Great Mosque of Samarra (848), built by Caliph Al-Mutawakkil, was the largest ever built, and its enormous heliconical (shell-spiral) minaret is one of the most spectacular in Islamic architecture.

Egypt had been invaded in the 7th century and the Mosque of 'Amr at Fustat (642), Cairo is the first of many Islamic buildings that traced the Arab route westward along the coast of North Africa. Among the most notable are the Ribat of Susah (810–21) in Tunisia, the Great Mosque of Qairouan (836), Tunisia, with its square minaret (a shape much copied, for example in the Giralda tower at Seville) perhaps inspired by ancient Graeco-Roman lighthouses. The Great Mosque of Ibn Tulun in Cairo, dating from 876, was modeled on the Samarra Mosque and in its time was one of the largest structures in the Nile valley.

The Susah Mosque, Tunisia, 9th century.

Mosque of Ibn Tulun, Cairo, Egypt, 9th century.

With the defeat of the Umayyads in 750 one member of their ruling family, Abd al-Rahman, escaped the slaughter and fled to Muslim Spain (al-Andalus) and founded his caliphate at Cordoba. In 785 he laid his plans for the Great Mosque of Cordoba which, with changes and additions over the following 200 years, became one of the great glories of Islamic architecture. By the early 11th century al-Andalus, battered by Christian attacks, was shattered into small warring Muslim principalities (Reinos de Taifas) which, despite civil wars, produced some wonderful architecture like the Aljaferiya, the palace fortress of Saragossa (1046–1081) which, behind its formidable fortifications, contains exquisitely refined interiors; the Toledo Synagogue (Santa Maria la Blanca), 1075–1085,

Cordoba Mosque, Spain, 8th century.

a symbol of Jewish-Arab co-existence, and the *bañuelos* (baths) of Granada.

The 10th century saw the rift in Islam between orthodox Sunnis and Shi'a which remains to this day. The Shi'ite Fatimids, in opposition to the ruling Sunni caliphate in Baghdad, invaded Egypt in 969 and created their fortified capital at Cairo where they also built the al-Azhar Mosque, a prime center of Muslim learning and the first theological university in the world.

S. Maria la Blanca, Toledo, Spain, 11th century.

In 1061 the Almoravid dynasty of fundamentalist Muslims was founded in the Maghreb (modern Morocco, Algeria, Tunisia) and, in 1110, invaded Spain. In 1147 they were followed there by the Almohads, also Berbers from North Africa, whose capital was Rabat. Both groups favored a sober, severe art that rejected any motif other than the purely abstract. Sharply pointed arches, sometimes scalloped, sometimes in *muqarnas* (stalactite) style, and the fortress-like exteriors of mosques combined to define the Hispano-Moorish style that spread throughout the Mahgreb and Andalusia. The Great Mosque of Seville (1171) has largely been lost under later Christian layers but the minaret, the Giralda Tower (so-called for the bronze angel that later topped its pinnacle), remains. One of the most impressive minarets of Almohad architecture towers 207ft/69m over the Kutbiyya Mosque (1195) in Marrakesh, Morocco.

By 1078/9 the Turkish Seljuks had established themselves in Damascus and Jerusalem (triggering the First Crusade of 1095) and in intense warfare that ensued, the architectural emphasis shifted toward fortification. In 1176 the great Saladin began work on a huge citadel just south of Cairo, using materials from the pyramids of Giza, and his brother built a protective wall around the old city of Damascus. At Aleppo in Syria, Saladin's son constructed a formidable castle (completed 1209) on the site of a Roman-Byzantine fortress. Although later destroyed by the Mongols and then again by Tamurlane, it was rebuilt by the Ottomans in the 16th century to the original specification.

The Seljuks were Sunni Muslims who were intent on spreading their version of Islam and to this end introduced a new type of architecture, *madrasas*, schools for the teaching of the Koran. The buildings combined two Persian forms: the *iwan* or covered area with one side opening through an arch to a courtyard, and muqarnas

decoration. One of the greatest examples is the Madrassa al-Firdaus in Aleppo (begun 1223).

By the late-13th century Egypt, the last refuge of Islamic culture against the Mongol invaders, had been successfully defended by the Mamluks. The Mosque and Madrasa of Sultan Hussan (begun 1356) marks a high point of early Mamluk architecture and the height of Cairo's medieval prosperity. The city owed much of its finest building to Sultan Qaitbay, particularly his madrasa (1472–4), described as "the ultimate achievement of architectural development in Cairo."

By the second half of the 14th century Islamic Spain was crumbling in the face of Christian advances but the two cultures were still intimately entwined. For example, the Alcazar of Seville (begun1364) was built for the Christian king Pedro I, but every detail, including the inscriptions, is Arabic. Only one minor Muslim dynasty, the Nasrids, survived in Spain until their expulsion in 1492, but their architectural legacy was extraordinary: the Alhambra, Granada (1338–90) is one of the most sumptuous of all Islamic palaces.

The Lion Court, Alhambra, Granada, Spain, 15th century.

The Ottoman expansion of the 14th–16th centuries enveloped a huge area, from Hungary in the north, Basra on the Persian Gulf to the south, North Africa, and Greece. But it was in Europe that their particular style of architecture emerged most fully. Before the fall of Constantinople (modern Istanbul) to the Ottomans in 1453, their capital was at Adrianopolis (modern Edirne, Turkey) and the Uch Sherefeli Mosque (1438–47) is considered the first building in a truly Ottoman style: interlocking arches of alternating colors, *muqarnas* decoration on capitals and door heads, and gently swelling lead-covered domes. Istanbul is full of major Ottoman buildings, some of the most outstanding being the Mosque of Beyazit (1501–8), the earliest surviving imperial mosque with its slim, multi-faceted minarets capped with tall steeples; Shezade Mosque (1544–48) built for Suleiman the Magnificent by the greatest Ottoman architect, Sinan; the Suleimaniye Mosque (1551–58) and Topkapu Serai, also by Sinan. It is in Edirne, however, that we find Sinan's masterpiece, the Selimiye Mosque (1569–74) with its eight huge piers carrying the largest dome in the Ottoman empire.

Beyazit Mosque, Istanbul, Turkey, 16th century.

Suleimaniye Mosque, Istanbul, Turkey, 16th century

13

GLOSSARY OF ARCHITECTURAL TERMS

(CHI) = Chinese
(ISL) = Islamic
(JAP) = Japanese
(HIN) = Hindu

Abacus
A slab forming the top member of a capital, usually square or curved-sided made of either stone or marble.

Ablaq (ISL)
Decorative system, that alternates dark and light layers, or white and black in stones or arch stones.

Abutment
Solid masonry that resists the lateral pressure or thrust of an arch.

Abutment.Bartholomew the Great, London, c.1123

Acanthus
A leaf form used in classical ornament.

Acropolis
Many ancient Greek cities were built on hills, the citadel at the top usually contained the principal temples and treasure-houses and the term implies some form of fortification.

Acroteria
Blocks resting on the vertex and lower extremities of a pediment to support statuary or ornaments.

Adobe
Brick dried in the sun, often used behind a facing of stone bricks as the core of a wall.

Adyton or adytum
The most sacred room of a Greek temple. Usually approached from the naos by a doorway.

Aedicule
A small temple like arrangement that became a oft-used motif in the Classical system: columns or pilasters carry a pedimented entablature and enframe a niche or window.

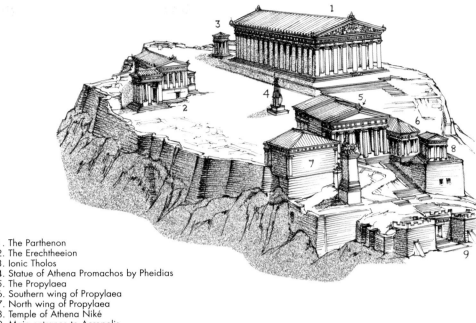

1. The Parthenon
2. The Erechtheeion
3. Ionic Tholos
4. Statue of Athena Promachos by Pheidias
5. The Propylaea
6. Southern wing of Propylaea
7. North wing of Propylaea
8. Temple of Athena Niké
9. Main entrance to Acropolis

The Acropolis, Athens, Greece

The term 'tabernacle' is sometimes used to express a similar meaning.

Agora
The Greek equivalent of the Roman forum, an open assembly generally a market.

Aisles
Lateral divisions parallel with the nave in a basilica or church.

Aisle of S. Lorenzo, Rome built AD 434 and 578.

Alabaster
A fine-grained, white, translucent gypseous mineral. Alabaster can be treated to simulate marble, a practice that evolved in Italy many centuries ago.

Alae
Small side alcoves, extensions or recesses opening from the atrium of a Roman house.

Alcazar
A Spanish term for a castle or fortress.

Alicatado
Uniformly sized glazed tiles used to cover a wall; common in Spain and Latin America.

Alcove
A large niche or recess set off from a room. Often arched, it is usually large enough to accommodate a bed or desk.

Alfiz (ISL)
Rectangular frame, slightly in relief, surrounding a horseshoe arch in an Islamic building.

Alveole (ISL)
A part of the 'honeycomb' structures forming stalactites. They were derived from the subdivision of pendentives into spherical triangles, corbelled one above the other. Alveoles gradually lost their structural character to become purely decorative.

Amalaka (HIN)
Horizontal disk with lateral ribs set at the top of a temple tower in Northern India.

Ambulatory
An aisle or covered passage that gives access between the choir, behind the altar and the apse of the church.

Andalus, al- (ISL)
Derived from 'vandalusie' or the country of the Vandals. This Arabic name was applied to all of Muslim Spain, after the barbarian invaders who had occupied the country.

American Order
The replacement of the acanthus-leaf decoration at the top of a Corinthian capital with traditional American motifs like corn-cobs, ears of corn, and tobacco leaves. First popularised by Benjamin Latrobe on the Capitol building, Washington DC (1793).

Amphitheater
A bowl-like walled space used for theatrical events and, during Roman times, gladiatorial games. The most notable example is the Colosseum, Rome (c. AD70).

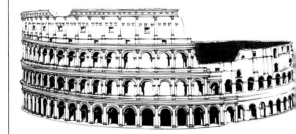

Amphitheater. The Colosseum, Rome, AD 70–82

14

Anta
A pilaster finishing the side wall of a Greek or Egyptian temple, with base and capital differing from those of adjacent columns.

Antechamber
A small room preceding a larger room, often used as a waiting area.

Antefixae
Carved blocks, fixed vertically at regular intervals along the lower edges of a roof in classical architecture.

Anthemion

Based on the honeysuckle flower, this classical ornament is seen in Greek and Roman architecture.

Apsara (HIN)
Celestial nymph often found among the carvings decorating a temple.

Apse
Semi-circular, or multangular termination of a church sanctuary. Most commonly to be found on the eastern or transeptal elevations. The apse is a continental feature that contrasts with the square termination of English Gothic churches.

Apse. S. Apollinare in Classe, Ravenna, Italy, AD 534–49

Aqueduct
A bridge-like structure with channels running the length of the top span to carry water over a valley, river bed, or road. The Pont-du-Gard (c. AD14) in southern France is one of the greatest examples of Roman aqueducts.

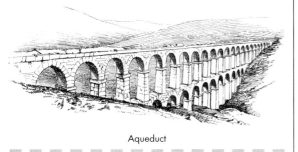
Aqueduct

Arabesque
A light and flowing surface decoration. Often decorated in flowers and leaves, it was often used by Arabic as well as Renaissance artists.

Arcade
A series of arches supported on piers or columns, attached to or detached from the wall.

Arch
A structure of wedge-shaped blocks over an opening. Designed to be held up when supported only from the sides.

Arch of Titus, Rome, AD 81

Architrave
The lowest division of the entablature. The word is also applied to the moulded frame around a door or window.

Arcuated construction
Whereby the structure is supported on arches.

Ardha-mandapa (HIN)
A form of vestibule to the main temple usually in the form of a small pillared hall. The northern temple style is known as antarala.

Arris
The vertical sharp edges formed by the meeting of two surfaces.

Art Deco
A style of European and American design that flourished in the 1920s and 1930s. Named after the Exposition International des Arts-Décoratifs et Industriel Modern in Paris, 1924–25. Much influenced by Egyptian style as well as Modernist preoccupations with speed, polished steel, and angularity. The Chrysler Building (1928–30) in New York is an outstanding example.

Art Nouveau
(France: Style Moderne; Germany Jugenstil; Italy, Floreale; Netherlands, Nieuwe Kunst)
Style of architecture and art that flourished in Europe and the USA from the late 19th century to the First World War. Characteristic features were motifs drawn from nature like entwined vines and flowers, or young women with flowing hair and gowns, all highly stylised. Guadi's Casa Battló (1905–7) in Barcelona is a good example.

Articulation
The designing, defining and dividing up of a façade into vertical and horizontal architectural members.

Art Deco. An advert for the Waldorf-Astoria hotel, New York City

☆ The Residence Apartments ☆
WALDORF ASTORIA

Arts and Crafts Movement
Late 19th century English movement influenced by William Morris among others. It sought to revive the skills and dedication of medieval craftmen in a world increasingly dominated by mindless automation and standardization. It had particular influence in the USA.

Ashlar
Hewn and squared masonry used as a building material.

Astragal
A small semi-circular moulding at the top of the column.

Atrium
In Early Christian and Byzantine architecture the term denoted an open square or courtyard. More commonly known as the entrance court or hall in Roman houses.

Atrium of S. Amrosio, Milan, Italy, c. 1140

Attic
A term applied in the Renaissance period to the upper story of a building above the main cornice.

Aula regia (ISL)
Audience chamber or throne room.

Avatar (HIN)
The incarnation of a deity, In Hinduism Krishna is regarded as an avatar of Vishnu.

Axis
The line that divides two symmetrical elements.

Balcony
A railed platform cantilevered out from a wall and usually supported by brackets, columns, or corbels. Access to the balcony is by window or door, often glazed.

Baldacchino
A canopy supported on pillars generally set over an altar or throne.

Baluster
A pillar or column supporting a handrail or coping.

Baptistery (upper building) of Pisa cathedral. Baptistery 1153–1278.

Baptistery
A building that contains the font for the baptismal rite.

Barbican
Exterior defense to a city or castle. Generally a double tower over a bridge or gate.

Baroque
A classical form of architecture prevalent in 17th and early 18th century Europe, originating in Italy. The words may derive from the Portuguese *barocco* meaning a misshapen pearl. The style is characterized by curved forms and a bold massing of large-scale shapes. The term was at first used in a derogatory sense, referring to curving, bizarre and bulbous shapes. The style is exuberant and theatrical employing swirls, sweeps, curves, and scrolls. There is sometimes exaggerated modelling in the service of religious zeal, especially in Italy and Spain. In France, Austria, Bavaria, and Bohemia it was less hysterical and tempered by classicism.

Baroque. Facade of the Cartuja church at Jerez de la Frontera, begun 1715

Barrel-vault
Like a barrel cut in half down its length, with one half used as an arch-like roof.

Basilica
Originally used in Roman architecture as a hall for the administration of justice. It was later adapted by the early Christians for their church designs. It was usually a rectangular building with an apse at one end. Inside it was divided into nave and aisles by columns supporting a timber roof.

Battlement
A parapet having a series of indentations or embrasures, between which are raised portions known as merlons.

Bauhaus
Literally 'building house'. A German school of design of great importance to modernist architecture in the 20th century. Walter Gropius became director in 1919 and the Bauhaus became the center of what is sometimes called the 'International Modern' style. In 1930 Mies van der Rohe became director with exacting standards of excellence and commitment. The Bauhaus was closed by the Nazis in 1933.

Bay
Compartments into which the nave or roof of a building is divided, it contrasts with the nave which is longitudinal. The term can also be used to describe projecting windows.

Bead
A cylindrical moulding often carved to resemble a string of beads.

Beaux-Arts
Originally a French late 18th century school of architecture based at the Ecole Nationale Supérieure des Beaux-Arts in Paris. However, the Beaux-Arts style flourished most strongly in France and America during the second half of the 19th century. The Opera House, Paris by Garnier is a good example of Beaux-Arts opulence and self-confidence.

Beaux-Arts. Opera House, Paris, 1858–64.

Bema
In Ancient Athens the term referred to a raised platform in a place of public assembly. It was later adapted by the Early Christians and used in their church design. It was generally at the apsidal end of a basilica for use by the clergy.

Belfry
The upper room of a tower in which the bells are hung. The term often applies to the tower itself.

Belverdere
Usually located at the roof-top of a dwelling, it is a roofed but open-sided structure affording an extensive view. The term can also refer to an independent building in a landscape or a formal garden.

Bogha-mandapa, Bogha-mandira (HIN)
Hall in which offerings were made.

Boss
the term refers to an ornament that projects at the intersection of the ribs of ceilings, whether vaulted or flat.

Brownstone
A popular building material in the 19th century in New York, this brown sandstone was found principally in New Jersey, Pennsylvania and Connecticut.

Buttress

A mass of masonry that is built against a wall to resist the pressure of an arch or a vault. The term flying buttress refers to an arch starting from a detached pier and abutting against a wall to take the thrust of the vaulting.

Angle buttress

Flying butttresses, Reims cathedral, France, 1210

Buyids (ISL)
dynasty of Shiite emirs, who occupied Baghdad in the tenth and eleventh century.

Byzantine architecture
In AD330 the Roman Emperor Constantine transferred the Imperial seat of government to Constantinople (modern Istanbul) originally a Greek city founded in 666BC. Byzantine architecture draws on this Greek foundation as well as Persia, Syria and Armenia. Brick was a prime building material; carved decoration was replaced by mosaic and marble cladding. The style reached its full flowering in the 6th century and influenced building styles in Italy, Russia, Greece, and throughout the Balkans.One of the greatest buildings of

Byzantine. St Mark's, Venice. Domes 13th century

Byzantine architecture is Hagia Sophia (AD532–7), Istanbul, and in western Europe St Mark's (begun 1042), Venice.

Caisson
Sunk panels, caissons or lacunaria sunk into a ceiling, dome or vault, often ornamented.

Caldarium
A hot room in a Roman Baths.

Caliph (ISL)
The caliph was the commander of the believers. He was the head of the Islamic community in the line of the Prophet's successors.

Campanile
The Italian word refers to a bell tower, generally detached from the main building.

Candrashala (HIN)
Northern Indian term that refers to an arch which is a barrel-vault seen in section. The symbolic role of the candrashala signifies the residence of the gods.

Campanile, Pisa, 1174–1350

Cantilever
A specially shaped beam that is supported securely at one end and carries a load distributed uniformly along the beam. The cantilever principle is frequently used in designs in of large bridges, e.g. the Forth Railway Bridge, near Edinburgh, Scotland.

Capital
The crowning feature of a column or pilaster.

Caravanserai
A large enclosed courtyard or inn for travellers.

Carrara marble
From the Carrara district in Tuscany, Italy. This snow-white marble was the favored medium of Michelangelo. The Romans knew it as Luna.

Cartouche
Ornament in the form of elaborate scrolls framing tablets and coats of arms.

Caryatid
In classical architecture, a female figure used as a support of an entablature. The term traditionally derived from the destruction of the city of Carya by the Greeks who then enslaved the women. The caryatid symbolizes the enslavement by depicting a woman who is condemned to hold up a building.

Casement
A strongly fortified chamber built into the thickness of a fortress wall. Today, the term applies other forms of armored enclosure, eg. gun turret.

Casement window
Opens on a hinge, like a door.

Caryatid

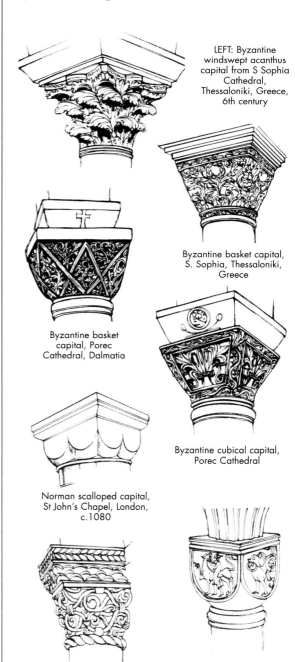

LEFT: Byzantine windswept acanthus capital from S Sophia Cathedral, Thessaloniki, Greece, 6th century

Byzantine basket capital, S. Sophia, Thessaloniki, Greece

Byzantine basket capital, Porec Cathedral, Dalmatia

Byzantine cubical capital, Porec Cathedral

Norman scalloped capital, St John's Chapel, London, c.1080

Norman cuchion capital, Leominster Priory, England

Romanesque carved wood capital, Urnes stave church, Norway, 1125–50

GLOSSARY OF ARCHITECTURAL TERMS

Casino
An ornamental garden or summer-house.

Cast-iron
Used largely in late 18th century building works, particularly bridges. Cast-iron was shaped by pouring the molten metal into moulds.

Cathedra
The chair or throne of a bishop in his cathedral church, originally placed in the apse behind the high altar.

Ceiling cove
Curved part of the ceiling where it meets the wall.

Cella
The enclosed, central part of an ancient temple.

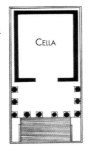

Cement
From the Latin *caementum*, 'rough stones'. In early times it referred to a mixture of broken stones held together by lime, clay, gypsum, and sand.

Centering
A structure set up to support a vault, ceiling or dome. Usually made of wood.

Chahr bagh (ISL)
A Persian term describing a garden surrounded by walls and divided by four waterways that represented the four rivers of Paradise.

Chaitya
Buddhist prayer hall, with apsidal ending; the barrel-vault forms the chaitya arch.

Chancel
Often referred to as the choir, this is the space for clergy and choir that is separated by a screen from the body of a church.

Chantry
A small chapel, generally attached to a church. It was often endowed with lands for the maintenance of priests who said, or originally sang, mass for the dead. The word derives from the Old French *chanterie* and the medieval Latin cantaria meaning to chant.

Chapel
From the Italian *cappella* meaning 'little cloak' in reference to the cloak of St Martin which was preserved by the Frankish kings as a saintly relic over which oaths could be sworn. In time the term came to be applied to a sanctuary in which holy relics were preserved. Early chapels were also known as oratories (places in which prayers could be said).

Chapterhouse
The chapter of a monastery or cathedral church is its governing and administrative body. This is where the members of the chapter met to discuss their ecclesiastical business.

Chashitsu (JAP)
A room within a house, or a small garden pavilion that was designed specifically for the tea ceremony.

Chevet
Term given to circular or polygonal apse when surrounded by an ambulatory from which radiate chapels.

Chevron
Ornament Romanesque decoration in zig-zag form.

Chigi
(JAP) The continuation of cross gable-end boards forming V-shape projections above the ridge of a Shinto shrine.

Choir
Area within a Christian church where the choir sings, usually at the eastern end near the altar.

Chumon (JAP)
The middle gate located between the outer south gate and the actual shrine or temple buildings.

Ciborium
Roman. A small building in the form of a canopy supported by columns.

Cimborio
The Spanish word for lantern or fenestrated cupola.

Clapboard
Sometimes called weatherboard. An exterior timber cladding usually of overlapping boards to provide insulation and weatherproofing.

Classical
The Latin word *classis* referred to the classes of Roman citizens and *classicus* denoted those who belonged to the highest class. During the Renaissance 'Classical' came to refer to the highest accomplishments of Ancient Greece and Rome in art, architecture, and literature.

Claustram
Moulded or finely-carved panel made of brick or wood openwork. It lets light in while filling an architectural space.

Clerestory
The upper story of a church generally pierced by a row of windows.

Cloisters
Covered passage round an open space, that connects the church to the chapter house, refectory and other parts of the monastery.

Cloister. Le Puy cathedral, France, 12th century

They were usually west of the transept and south of the nave, probably to secure sunlight.

Coffer
Sunken panels in a ceiling, vault or dome, also known as caissons or lacunae (literally 'holes'). In classical architecture they may be square, hexagonal, octagonal, or diamond-shaped.

Coffered ceiling, the Pantheon, Rome, AD120

Colonnade
A row of columns supporting an entablature or arches.

Column
A vertical support, generally consisting of base, circular shaft, and spreading capital. Pairs of columns are described as coupled An engaged, applied, or attached column is one where part of the column's surface makes contact with the wall. In a half or demi column.

Conch
The domed ceiling of a semi-circular apse.

Concrete
From the Latin *concretus*, 'grown or run together'. One of the oldest building materials, it is composed of sand, cement, and stone, and water. The first two ingredients are inert but the cement and water form a chemical bond turning the whole into a rock-hard conglomerate. The earliest examples date from 5600BC and concrete was certainly used by the Ancient Egyptians. The Romans used it extensively, using volcanic earth from the region of Pozzuoli near Vesuvius. They also experimented with concrete reinforced with bronze strips. They built massive walls and vaults with pozzolana concrete, the Colosseum in Rome being an famous example.

Coping
The protective capping or covering to a wall designed to shed water.

Corbel
A block of stone, projecting from a wall, supporting the beams of a roof, floor vault or other feature, it is often elaborately carved or moulded.

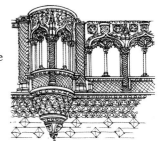

Corbel

Corbelling
Courses built out beyond one another generally to support roofs, vaults and domes. Creating a pyramidal roof.

Corbel table
A projecting section of wall supported by a range of corbels and forming a parapet crowned by a coping.

Corinthian
The Corinthian Order has a fluted shaft and a bell-shaped capital, from which eight acanthus stalks (*caulicoli*) emerge to support the moderate volutes.

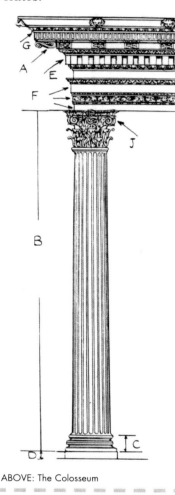

CORINTHIAN
A Modillion
B Column
C Base
D Plinth
E Dentil
F Fascia
G Corona
H Tenia
I Hypotrachelium
J Volute

ABOVE: The Colosseum

Cornice
A moulded projection which crowns a wall, building or arch. In classical architecture it represents the top member of the entablature.

Cortile
The Italian name for the internal court which is surrounded by an arcade.

Cour d'honneur
The finest court of a great house or château, where visitors were formally received.

Crenellation
an opening in the upper part of the parapet furnished with indentations or 'crenelles'.

Crocket
A projecting block of stone carved with foliage to decorate the raking lines formed by angles of Gothic spires and canopies.

Crossing
Central area of nave, chancel and transepts.

Above this lofty space is generally set a tower or a cupola.

Cruciform
A plan based on the form of a cross.

Crypt
A space in churches, generally beneath the chancel, and used for burial in early times.

Cul-de-four
Roof in the form of a semidome at the corners of a cupola resting on pendentives or above a niche.

Cupola
A spherical roof, placed like an inverted cup over a square, circular or multiangular apartment.

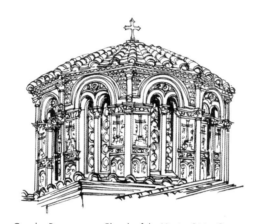

Cupola. Romanesque Church of the Virgin, Stiris, Greece

Curtain wall
In modern architecture this term describes external walls that serve no load-bearing purpose but are suspended on the face of a building like a curtain. Generally composed of repeated modular elements such as glass in metal framing.

Cusp
Point forming the foliations in Gothic tracery.

Cyclopean
Masonry walling composed of immense blocks of masonry, named after the Cyclops. Examples can be seen in the buildings at Mycenae, Crete.

Cyma
Used in classical architecture especially, the term refers to a moulding in a section of two contrasting curves - either cyma recta or cyma reversa.

Decorated
Prevalent during the 14th century, the term refers to the style of English Gothic architecture.

Dentil
Classical form of ornament 'like teeth' in Ionic and Corinthian cornices.

Deul (HIN)
Used especially in Northern India, the name refers to the tower of a temple or the whole layout.

Divan (ISL)
Persian term that designated the sovereign's council of state. A distinction was made between the chamber for public audiences with the prince and the private audience room used during courtly ceremonies. The formula of the two courtyards developed further under the Romans and Sassanids, evolving into many forms of Arab courtyards.

Diwan-i-am (HIN)
The hall for public audiences in a Indian Moghul palace.

Diwan-i-khas (HIN)
Hall for private audiences in an Indian Moghul palace.

Dome
A convex covering, usually hemispherical or semi-elliptical over a circular or polygonal space.

Domus
Roman private house.

Donjon
The inner great tower, or keep, of a castle.

Donjon (central tower)

Doric
The shaft is fluted with the capital plain. The Doric order is unique in having no base to the column.

Doric Order. Temple of Zeus, Olympia, Greece, c.460BC

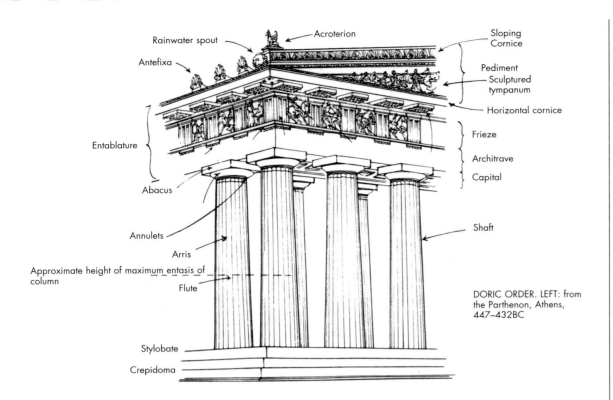

Labels: Rainwater spout, Acroterion, Sloping Cornice, Antefixa, Pediment, Sculptured tympanum, Horizontal cornice, Entablature, Frieze, Architrave, Capital, Abacus, Shaft, Annulets, Arris, Approximate height of maximum entasis of column, Flute, Stylobate, Crepidoma

DORIC ORDER. LEFT: from the Parthenon, Athens, 447–432BC

Dormer
A window in a sloping roof, usually that of a sleeping apartment.

Dosseret
A deep block sometimes placed above the Byzantine capital to support the wide voussoirs of the arch above.

Dravidian *(hin)*
The architectural style of Southern India, named after the group of languages spoken in southern and central India.

Dressings
Worked and finished stones used in architectural features such as doorways and window openings.

Drum
The circular or poly-sided vertical walling supporting a dome, in which windows might be placed to light the central area of a building.

Dvarapala (HIN)
Symbolic guardian of the gates of a Buddhist, Jain or Hindu temple.

Early English
The style, prevalent during the 13th century, of English Gothic architecture.

Eaves
The lower part of a roof that projects beyond the face of the wall.

Echinus
A curved or projected moulding supporting the abacus of the Doric order. The curve resembles the shell of a sea-urchin and the name is derived from the Greek for sea-urchin.

Egyptian Revival
A style originated in 18th century France reflecting the revived interest in things Egyptian following Napoleon's Egyptian campaigns and the growth of Egyptian archaeology. The clarity of line and austerity of form played an important part in Neoclassicism.

Elizabethan
The building style of the reign of Elizabeth I of England (1558-1603). It was a time of extensive building, particularly of for the aristocracy and merchant class, and a stylistic transition between late Gothic and the Renaissance.

Engaged column
In classical architecture, a column which is attached to the wall so that only a half to three-quarters of its circumference is visible.

Entablature
Horizontal, lintel-like slab supported by columns.

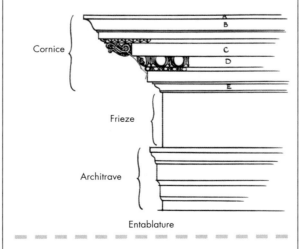

Labels: Cornice, Frieze, Architrave, Entablature

Entasis
A swelling or curving outwards along the line of a column shaft. Designed to counteract the optical illusion which gives a shaft bounded by straight lines the appearance of curving inwards. It is derived from the Greek word distension.

Façade
The face or elevation of a building.

Fan Vault
Vaulting in which all the ribs have the same curve, and resemble the framework of a fan. This vaulting was characteristic to the Perpendicular Gothic period.

Fillet
A flat, narrow band that separates column flutes and divides mouldings from one another.

Finial Ornament
Finishing off the upper portion of a gable, roof, bench-end or other architectural feature.

Flamboyant
A phase of French Gothic (late 13th-mid-16th centuries). The word derives from the French *flammes* – flames – which describes the style of tracery.

Flèche
From the French word meaning 'shaft' or 'arrow'. A slender wooden or metal spire generally found over the crossing on a Gothic church. It was widely used in French churches because it caused fewer problems of stress and thrust than a tower. A classic example is that of Notre-Dame, Paris.

Flèche. Central spire of Notre Dame cathedral, Paris, 1180–1330

Flute
Vertical channelling in the shaft of a column.

Folly
A purely decorative building set in a picturesque landscape garden or park. Often a faux-medieval ruin or a Chinese pagoda. Particularly popular in France, England and the USA during the 18–19th centuries.

Font
A dish-like vessel in the nave of a Christian church, usually of stone, that contains consecrated water for baptism. Some examples have elaborate carved wooden covers.

Forum
The public space used for markets, courts of justice and business in every Roman town.

Fret ornament
Classical decoration consisting of an assemblage of straight lines intersecting at right angles, and of various patterns.

Frieze
The central division of the classical entablature.

Frigidarium
The large, cold water swimming bath of a Roman bath.

Frontispiece
The two-or-three stage entrance feature applied to the main façade of a building or court.

Fusuma (JAP)
Interior partitions that are made of a latticework wood frame and are covered with heavy opaque paper.

Gable
The triangular upper part of the end wall of a building which rises to the slopes of a pitched roof. The entire wall is known as a gable end.

Gallery
(a) A long narrow chamber or passage constructed above the aisle of a church. In many churches there is a gallery at the west end to contain an organ loft; (b) In medieval halls a minstrel's gallery was built at the opposite end to the dais at which the lord and lady sat; (c) an apartment for the display of painting and sculpture; (d) the upper tier of seats in a theater.

Garbha griha (HIN)
The shrine or sanctum of the temple.

Gargoyle
A decorative stone water spout originally on medieval buildings, particularly cathedrals. It was often carved into grotesque animal or human forms.

Gatehouse
A protective entrance gateway on medieval castles, grand houses, abbeys and fortified towns.

Gazebo
A pavilion or summer house usually set on rising ground within the gardens of a grand house.

Georgian
English and American architecture of mainly classical design built during the reigns of the four king Georges of England, a period covering 1714–1830.

Ghanta Kalasha (HIN)
Emblematic bell-shaped vase set on the roof of a Hindu temple

Giant order
Also known as colossal order, it consists of columns and pilasters extending through two or more stories of a façade.

Gopuram (HIN)
Access to a Dravidian temple precinct in the form of a monumental gateway.

Gothic
The style of building current in Europe between the later 12th century and the middle of the 16th century. Gothic architecture is characterized by the pointed arch, the ribbed vault, flying buttresses,

Gothic. Norwich cathedral, England, 1096-1120. Spire c. 1464–72

traceried windows, slender piers, and lofty steeples. Although some of these features were used in different parts of the world at an earlier date it is the fusion of all of them into delicate yet strong structures that creates a Gothic building. The emphasis is on height, in contrast to Classical Greece and Rome with their emphasis on the horizontal entablature. The term 'Gothic' was first used by Giorgio Vasari, the Renaissance Italian artist and historian, who used it to denote something crude and barbaric – made by the Goths.

Gothic Revival
A romantic and nostalgic architectural movement (mainly in England and to a lesser extent the USA) that had started in the late 18th century but became an important trend from about 1840. One of the most outstanding examples is the Palace of Westminster, London built between 1836 and 1865 by Sir Charles Barry and A.W.N. Pugin

Gothic Revival. St Pancras station and hotel, London, 1863–75

Greek cross plan
A cruciform plan where the four arms of the cross are of equal length.

Greek Revival
Inspired by archeological finds in Greece and Italy as well as the romanticism generated by the Greek War of Independence. Widely adopted in USA, England, Prussia, and

Bavaria. A good example is von Schinkel's Altes Museum (1824–8), Berlin.

Guilloche
Classical ornament in the form of an intertwined plait, frequently used to ornament the 'torus' moulding.

Gumpha (HIN)
Word meaning cave, used particularly in association with the caves of Orissa, India.

Gymnasium
A place for physical exercise and training in Ancient Greece.

Half-timber building
A building, usually a house, of timber posts, struts and rails. The interspaces are filled with brick or are sometimes plastered. Western Europe, particularly Britain 15-17th centuries and 17th and early 18th century Colonial America.

Half-timbering. The Guildhall, Lavenham, England, c.1529

Hall Church
A rectangular church, generally of Gothic design, in which the nave and aisles are of equal height. Most commonly found in Scandinavia and Germany.

Hamam (ISL)
Following the model of Roman baths, these are public or private baths.

Haniwa (JAP)
Minature clay models of houses and figures found in ancient tombs and imperial burial mounds.

Haram (ISL)
Usually a prayer hall, it is a consecrated space in a mosque where rituals and prayers take place. The term can also be applied to an entire sacred area such as the Temple Mound on Mount Moriah.

Herm
Statue composed of a human bust joined to a tapering quadrangular pedestal. Found in ancient Greece and Rome, it was revived in the Renaissance and 18th century and used extensively as a garden ornament.

Hippodrome
A course for horse or chariot racing, in Ancient Greece it was the equivalent to the Roman circus.

Hisashi (JAP)
Covered verandas or corridors that are attached to the main rooms of a dwelling.

Honden (JAP)
The main sanctuary building of a Shinto shrine which holds the representation of the deity.

Horseshoe arch (ISL)
An upper stilted arch with the stonework between the imports and the springing line resembling stilts.

Hôtel-particulier
Grand French townhouse usually consisting of an arched gateway leading to a courtyard. The main house was often flanked by wings.

Hoysala (HIN)
Describes the highly ornamental architecture typical of the southern Deccan in India.

Hypocaust
An underfloor chamber of brick or stone in ancient Roman buildings for heating. Hot air from the basement furnace passed through wall flues to heat all the rooms. The term is derived from the two Greek words meaning 'the place heated from below').

Hypostyle
A pillared hall in which the roof rests on columns, also applied to the many columned halls of Egyptian temples.

Impost
The slightly protruding block of stone which supports the springer of one arch in an arcade.

Insula
A Roman multi-storyed tenement block.

Intercolumniation
The space between two columns.

International Style
An architectural school originating with Walter Gropius and others at the Bauhaus in Germany just after the First World War. It is characterized by austere cubes and undecorated surfaces. Simplicity and functionality were guiding principles. It became a benchmark style for much modern building after the Second World War throughout western Europe and the USA.

Intersecting vault
Where two vaults intersect at right angles. Most often seen in the crossing of a church where the transepts cross nave and choir.

Intrados
The curved inner surface of a vault or an arch.

Ionic
Light and elegant with slim columns that are generally fluted, It is distinguished principally by the volutes of its capital.

Iwan (ISL)
Originating in Iran the vaulted architectural space usually has an open façade. The iwan is characteristic of Islamic art influenced by Persia.

Jacobean
English architecture during the reign of James I (1603–25). A continutation of Elizabethan, the style blended Italian Renaissance and Flemish influences.

Jagamohana (HIN)
The name of the assembly or dance hall in Hindu temples of Orissa, India.

Jali (HIN)
Created by piercing a slab of stone in imitation of lattice work that allows some light to filter into the building while blocking a bay.

Jodan (JAP)
A raised area in a room on which tokonama, tana and shoin are usually placed, designating the most important area of the room.

Ionic Order. Temple of Fortuna Virilis, Rome, 1st century BC

Kaaba (ISL)
Sacred centre of Islam in Mecca. The Koran decrees that every Muslim makes the journey to Mecca at least once in their lifetime.

Kalasha (HIN)
Emblematic water vessel that crowns the tower of a temple.

Kasr (ISL)
A fortified palace or castle in the desert.

Katsuogi (JAP)
Tapered wood cylinders along the ridges of a Shinto shrine buildings.

Keep
The inner great donjon or tower of a castle.

Keystone
The central stone of a semicircular arch.

Kiosk
A light, open pavilion.

Kokoshniki
Russian term for series in arches set in rows that is often seen in Byzantine constructions.

Kondo (JAP)
The 'Golden Hall' within a Buddhist temple that houses the most sacred images.

Kuan (CHI)
Watch tower.

Kudu (HIN)
Referring to the residence of the Gods, this is a term for the chaitya arch and is often highly decorated with a bust-length figure in it.

Lady-chapel
A subsidiary chapel within a large church devoted to the Virgin Mary

Lakhmids (ISL)
Dynasty of pre-Islamic Arab princes in Iraq, 4th Century AD.

Lantern
A small circular or polygonal structure mounted on top of a dome or hall roof allowing light into the main structure.

Leitmotif
A recurrent decorative theme

Lych (or lich) gate
A sheltered gateway to a churchyard. Used as a resting place for a coffin during the funeral service.

Linga (HIN)
The symbolic phallus of Shiva often found in the sanctum of a Shivaite temple.

Lintel
A horizontal slab of stone or wood spanning an opening such as a doorway and supporting the wall above it.

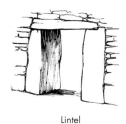

Lintel

Loggia
Open sided gallery or colonnade.

Lunette
A semicircular window let into the inner base of a concave dome or vault.

Machicolation
A defensive feature in some castles and fortified houses where a parapet, supported on corbels, projected from the wall with an opening in the floor allowing the defenders to pour boiling oil or drop stones on to the attackers below.

Madrasa (ISL)
The madrasa was extensively followed during the era of the Seljuks. It is a Koranic shool whose architectural form follows the tradition of mosques, with Persian-style courtyards containing iwans.

Mahadeva (HIN)
The Great God, epithet of Shiva, is also applied to Vishnu.

Mahal (HIN)
Palace.

Maha-mandapa (HIN)
Vestibule in southern Indian temple style.

Mandala (HIN)
The circle as a symbolic diagram consisting of circles and rectangles representing the world in its cosmic development.

Mandapa (HIN)
Columned hypostyle hall in a Hindu temple, where the ritual dances take place.

Mandira (HIN)
the North Indian term for the Mandapa.

Mannerism
Architectural style dating from the period of Michelangelo (1475–1564) to the end of the 16th century. It used classical elements in a deliberately 'abnormal' way and often in opposition to their original context.

Manoeline
Named after the Portuguese king Dom Manoel I, a decorative architectural style in the 16th century.

Mansard roof
A roof with a flatter upper portion and a steep lower slope, also known as a 'gambrel' roof.

Martyrium
Christian sanctuary dedicated to a martyr.

Masjid (ISL)
Mosque.

Masqura (ISL)
Enclosed area around the most sacred part of the mosque where the sovereign attended prayers.

Mastaba
Used to cover a burial chamber, this ancient Egyptian word describes a rectangular, flat topped funerary mound.

Mausoleum
A monumental building to house a tomb or tombs usually of dignitaries. Named after the Mausoleum of Harlicarnassos (modern Bodrum, Turkey) which was built by King Mausolus for his wife Artemisia who died in 353BC.

Maydan (ISL)
Large open spaces often used for army parades and victory marches.

Metope
The space between Doric triglyphs. Commonly decorated with sculptured groups or carved ornaments.

Mezzanine
An intermediate floor built within a lofty storey.

Mihrab (ISL)
Niche in the qibla wall that indicates the direction of Mecca. The mosque's holy of holies it forms a small internal space preceded by an arch.

Minaret
A slender tower above a mosque, from which the muezzin calls the faithful to prayer.

Minbar (ISL)
Raised seat or pulpit in a mosque from which the cleric addresses the congregation.

Misericord
Literally a 'mercy seat' A hinged seat, designed to support a standing person, often a member of the choir, who was obliged by the liturgy to stand for long periods of time. The underside is often carved with grotesques.

Mithuna (HIN)
Depiction of amorous couple, often found sculpted in temple decoration.

Modillion
A small bracket that supports a cornice or corbel.

Module
A unit of measurement, by which the parts of a classical order or building are regulated. Generally taken from the half-diameter of a column at its junction with the base.

Moghul *or* **Mogul**
Indian Islamic architecture of the 16–18th centuries. The Taj Mahal (1631–53) is probably the best-known example.

Monolithic column
A column whose shaft is made from one piece of stone or marble as opposed to one made up in hollow drums.

Moorish
Term used to describe Islamic architecture of North Africa and the Iberian peninsula during the time of the Arab occupation (AD711–1492). The Alhambra, Grenada, Spain, is a famous example.

Mosaic
Small cubes made from marble, stone or glass. Used to make up decorative surfaces.

Motte
The earthen conical mound of a castle. Motte-and-bailey castles were a common form before c.1100. The bailey was an area of land surrounding the motte, itself protected by a wall or palisade.

Mouldings
The contours given to projecting members.

Moya (JAP)
The central interior space of a Shinden.

Mudejar
A style of Spanish architecture, particularly of Castile and Aragon, that blends Christian and Muslim characteristics. It was mainly seen between 12th–16th centuries but survived into the 17th century.

Mullions
The vertical divisions in windows that separates them into different number of lights.

Muqarnas (ISL)
Characteristic of Islamic architecture, these decorative stalactites adorn the cupolas or corbels of a building.

Mushrabeyeh (ISL)
The wooden lattice-work in the upper windows of Islamic houses.

Mutule
Blocks attached under Doric cornices from which the guttae depend.

Nagara (HIN)
Refers to the architectural style of North-East India.

Nageshi (JAP)
Resembling a beam between posts, this horizontal wooden plank is usually near the top of the room.

Nandi (HIN)
A bull, the vehicle of Shiva.

Naos
The inner sanctum of a Greek temple that contained the cult statue. In Byzantine churches it refers to the sanctuary.

Nata-mandira (HIN)
The dance hall of a Northern Indian style temple.

Narthex
Area within Early Christian and Byzantine churches sectioned off for women and penitents.

Nave
Longitudinal areas in a covered building. Naves are often formed by arcades perpendicular to the qibla.

Nave. Abbey church of Fontevrault, France, 1104–50

Necking
The space between the astragal of a column shaft and the actual capital.

Necropolis
A burial ground.

Neoclassicism
Late 18th century, early 19th century in Germany, France, Britain, and the USA. The severe classicism of Ancient Greece and Rome was an inspiration and an antidote to the high decoration of the Baroque and Rococo. The 18th century saw the foundation of modern archaeology and this was also a powerful stimulus.

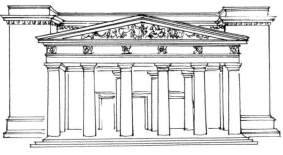

Neoclassicim. Neue Wache, Berlin, 1816

Niche
A recess in a wall, often used to place a statue or an ornament.

Obelisk
A tall, square section of pillar that tapers upwards and ends in a pyramid.

Odeion
A building designed for musical contests, resembling a Greek theater.

Oeillet
From the French *oeil*, eye. The slit in the walls of medieval castles through which arrows could be fired.

Orchestra
The space in a Greek theater where the chorus sang and danced.

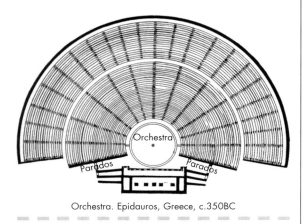

Orchestra. Epidauros, Greece, c.350BC

Order
In architecture, an order comprises a column with a shaft, capital and usually a base.

Pada (HIN)
The base of a building, typical of eastern Indian temples.

Paga (HIN)
Vertical projection on a temple tower.

P'ai-lou (CHI)
Commemorative or decorative arch, often with 1–3 or 5 openings.

Pancayatana (HIN)
Hindu word describes a group of 5 temples. One central temple surrounded by 4 smaller shrines.

Panelling
The practice of lining the interior walls with wooden boards became widespread in western Europe during the 13th century but reached its most decorative level in the 16th and 17th centuries.

Parapet
Seen in platforms, bridges and balconies, the portion of wall above the roof-gutter that is sometimes battlemented.

Patio
A Spanish arcaded or colonnaded courtyard.

Pavilion
A projecting part of a façade of a building, usually at the ends or centre. The term is also applied to a small ornamental building in a garden.

Pedestal
Usually made up of a base, die, cornice or cap-mould, and used as a support for a statue, column or vase.

Pediment
A triangular piece of wall above the entablature, enclosed by raking cornices, seen in classical architecture.

Pendentive
The term applied to the spherical triangles formed by the intersecting of the dome by two pairs of opposite arches, themselves supported over a square or polygonal compartment.

Peribolus (ISL)
Consecrated area, defined by a wall or enclosure that surrounds a church or temple.

Peristyle
A row of columns that surrounds a cloister, temple or court. It also describes the area that is enclosed.

Piano nobile
In classical building it is the first and principal floor of the house.

Piazza
Describes an open, public space that is surrounded by buildings.

Peristyle

Pidas (HIN)
Series of superimposed corbels, typical of the step-roofs of Mandapas.

Pier
A mass of masonry from which an arch springs, in a bridge or an arcade.

Pier

Pilaster
A rectangular feature in the shape of a pillar often engaged in the wall.

Greek Doric: Temple of Hephaistos (The Thesion). Athens, c. 449BC

Greek Ionic: The Erechtheion, Athens, c. 421BC

Greek Corinthian: Monument of Lysicrates, Athens, c. 334BC

Greek Doric in Italy: Temple of Athena, Paestum, 510BC

Roman Doric: Theater of Marcellus, Rome, 23–13BC

Roman Ionic: Temple of Fortuna Virilis, Rome, 2nd century BC

Comparative Orders

24

Pilaster strip
Low relief vertical strips with the appearance of pilasters. They have solely decorative purposes.

Pilotis
Derived from the French word for pile or stake. A term used in modern architecture to describe buildings that stand supported on columns and piers.

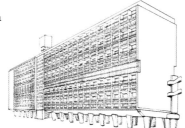

Pilotis. Unite d'Habitation, Marseilles, France, 1946–52

Piscina
A stone water basin usually set into a niche near the altar of a Christian church. They were used for washing the vessels used in the Mass or Communion.

Pishtaq (ISL)
A large rectangular screen that frames an Islamic iwan, also the gateway to a mosque or mausoleum.

Pita deul (HIN)
The meeting or dance pavilion.

Plateresque
A term used to describe an intricate style named after its likeness to silver-work. This phase of Spanish architecture took place between 15th and 16th centuries.

Plinth
The projected or moulded base of any building, it is also the lowest square member of the base of a column.

Podium
A continuous projecting base or pedestal. It also describes the enclosing platform of the arena of the amphitheater.

Porphyry
A red or purple rock used as a building stone or sculpture, particularly by the Greeks, Egyptians and Romans.

Portcullis
A heavy latticed wooden or iron gate in the portal of a defended building that could be raised and lowered.

Portico
A colonnaded space that forms a vestibule or entrance, with a roof supported on at least one side by columns.

Portico. The Pantheon, Rome, AD120

Porte-cochère
Usually applied to a canopy projecting beyond the main entrance of a grand house of the 19th century. The canopy was large enough to shelter a carriage from rain.

Post-Modernism
A group of, mainly, American architects like Philip Johnson, Michael Graves, Robert Stern, and Robert Venturi, who rejected the rationality of Bauhaus modernism in favor of an eclectic architectural vocabulary, sometimes playful, sometimes kitchy. Where Mies van der Rohe, the quintessential modernist, had proclaimed "less is more", Robert Venturi countered with "less is a bore".

Pradakshinapatha (HIN)
The passageway around a shrine that the devotee walked as part of the ritual of worship.

Presbytery
The area of a Christian church containing the high altar. Also refers to a priest's house.

Pronaos
The vestibule of a Greek or Roman temple.

Propylaeum
In Greek architecture this referred to an important gateway or entrance. A famous example is is the propylaeum on the Acropolis hill in Athens leading to the temple area.

Putto
From the Italian word meaning child, describes the baby and cherub sculptures on Baroque architecture.

Pylon
Describes the mass of masonry with a central opening, forming a monumental entrance to Egyptian temples.

Qasr (ISL)
A palace, castle or mansion.

Qibla (ISL)
The wall of mosque which is oriented towards Mecca. During prayer the faithful prostrate themselves towards the Qibla.

Quoin
From the French *coin*, 'corner' or 'angle'. Quoins or quoin-stones are the dressed stones forming the angle of two joining exterior walls.

Quoin

Qubba (ISL)
Originally referred to a domed building, has come to mean a Islamic mausoleum or tomb.

Ramma (JAP)
Decoratively carved panels above sliding fusuma doors.

Rampart
An earthen bank that surrounds a fortress, castle or fortified city, used as a defense.

Ratha (HIN)
The word has two meanings, the first refers to a chariot in the form of a movable temple that were used to transport images of the gods during festivals. The second meaning is a generic term for the projections on temple towers.

Refectory
The dining-hall of a convent, monastery or college.

Rekha (HIN)
In Orissa the word means the tower of a temple.

Relieving arch
A slab or relieving arch is constructed to stop the weight of masonry above from crushing the lintel stone below.

Renaissance
From the Italian *Rinascimento* and the French *renaître*, both meaning 're-born'. What the rebirth refers to is the rediscovery of the glories of Ancient Greece and Rome by Italian scholars, artists and architects in the 15th century. The impact of these discoveries had a profound effect on European and American architecture for 400 years.

Retablo
A Spanish word that is used to describe a framing or altarpiece that encloses painted panels above a church altar.

Rib
A projecting-band on a ceiling or vault.

Ribat (ISL)
A fortified monastery often found on the frontiers of the Islamic empire.

Rococo
A highly romantic style, elegant, playful and light, that originated in France and Italy in the 18th century but was also adopted brilliantly in southern Germany.

Nave vault
Clerestory window
Triforium arcade
Triforium passage
Vaulting shaft which divides the bays
Nave arcade
Nave capital
Aisle window
Nave column
Wall arcading

Romanesque. Durham Cathedral, England, 1093

Romanesque
An architectural style flourishing between the 7th and 12th centuries AD in those areas of Europe originally part of the Roman Empire. Characterized by basilica or circular-form churches, rounded arches with strongly carved decoration, sturdy cylindrical piers, thick walls, and simple barrel-vaulted ceilings. A classic example is the nave of Durham cathedral, England, begun 1093.

Rotunda
A building with a circular ground plan and often topped by a dome.

Rustication
Stones used in a building's façade (often on the lower storeys of Renaissance and Mannerist buildings) where the face of the stone protrudes and has been roughened to contrast with the smooth surface of the rest of the façade.

Set-off
A horizontal member that connects the lower and thicker part of a wall with the receding upper part.

Sgraffito
A form of decoration where the upper coat of white stucco is partly cut away to show a dark undercoat so forming a design.

Shaft
The portion of column between the base and the capital.

Shala (HIN)
The name of the small arches that decorate the rooftops of Dravidian temples.

Shikhara (HIN)
The tower of a temple

Shinden (JAP)
The chief building of a Heian Period mansion-estate.

Shingle style
External walls that are clad in shingles (wooden tiles) over a timber frame.

Shitomido (JAP)
paper-covered wood lattice 'doors', they can be swung up horizontally and hooked open. They form the front of Shinden buildings.

Shoin (JAP)
A desk alcove that projects out onto the veranda, with a shoji window above it.

Shoji (JAP)
Outer partition doors that are made of latticework wood frame and covered with translucent white paper.

Shrine
A sanctuary dedicated to a Christian martyr, the martyrium generally had a central plan with a cupola.

Shthapaka (HIN)
The Hindu word for the architect who designs the temples according to the ritual requirements.

Shthapati (HIN)
The architect who carries out the plan of the shthapaka.

Soffit
The underside or ceiling of any architectural member.

Span
The distance between the supports of a roof, beam or arch.

Spandrel
Triangular space enclosed by the curve of an arch and the rectangle of outer mouldings as in a doorway.

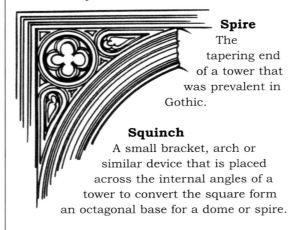

Spire
The tapering end of a tower that was prevalent in Gothic.

Squinch
A small bracket, arch or similar device that is placed across the internal angles of a tower to convert the square form an octagonal base for a dome or spire.

Stave church
The medieval wooden churches of Scandanavia.

Steeple
A tower topped by a spire.

Stilted arch
An arch that has its springing arch higher than the line of the impost mouldings. It is then connected by vertical pieces of walling or stilts.

Stoa
A portico or detached colonnade found in Ancient Greek architecture.

Strapwork
A type of relief ornament that resembles leather straps, intertwined and forming panels. Especially used in early Mannerist type renaissance work in Britain and the Low Countries.

String course
A moulding or projecting course running along the elevation of a building.

Stucco
A plaster covering applied to masonry or brickwork that is sometimes moulded to imitate architectural features like cornices. It was used by ancient Roman and Islamic builders but reached its most sophisticated forms during the Renaissance, Baroque, and Rococo.

Stupa (HIN)
A funeral mound that symbolises the presence and law of Buddha.

Stupi (HIN)
A rounded finial section of a Dravidian temple.

Stylobate
The upper step forming a platform on which a colonnade is placed, seen in Greek temple design.

Sudare (JAP)
Horizontal roll-up bamboo blinds made of thin bamboo strips.

Sukiya (JAP)
A chashitsu or inner room for the elaborate tea ceremony.

T'a
Chinese term (perhaps derived from the Indian stupa) for a pagoda.

Tainoya (JAP)
Pavilions that are located on either side of a central house and contain subsidary living quarters.

Tantra (HIN)
Religious writings that deal with ritual and symbolism.

Tatami (JAP)
A rectangular floor mat made of rush, measuring approximately six-by-three feet and about two inches thick, the edges are bound by cloth strips.

Tateana (JAP)
Prehistoric thatch-roofed pit dwellings.

Temenos
Greek word for a sacred space or an urban area consecrated to a deity.

Tempietto
The term is usually reserved for Renaissance and later buildings of an ornamental character. Temple-like structures, they were often erected in parks and and gardens of country houses.

Tepidarium
Room in Roman baths that is of moderate heat.

Stoa of Attalos, Athens, c. 150BC

Terracotta
The baked and glazed earthenware used in the decoration of exterior and interior walls, as well as floors.

Tessarae
Cubes made from glass, marble or semi-precious material that are used to create a mosaic.

Tholos
Greek word for a circular building with a domed or conical roof. Remains of tholoi survive at Olympia, Epidauros, Delphi, and Athens.

Tie-beam
Generally the lowest member of a roof truss, it extends from wall plate to wall plate and is intended to prevent the walls from spreading.

Tien (CHI)
Hall.

Tie Rod
A metal or wooden strut that connects the imposts of an arcade to brace an architectural structure and to ensure stability.

Tokonoma (JAP)
A recessed alcove in a room that is used for displaying paintings, ceramics or flower arrangements.

Torana (HIN)
A portal with a monolithic or lintelled arch that is set befor a Buddhist or Hindu arch.

Torii (JAP)
The entrance gate to a Shinto shrine.

Trabeated construction
A structure that is composed of horizontal lintels and vertical posts.

Tracery
The 'veins' or ribs of stonework that sub-divide windows, screens, panels, or ceilings of Gothic buildings.

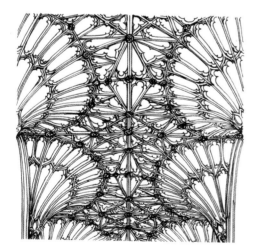
Tracery

Transept
Set at right angles to the nave and choir, transepts are the arms of a cruciform church.

Travertine
A porous Italian stone with a yellowish appearance.

Trefoil arch
A triple arch having three concave sections.

Triconch or Triple apse
Seen largely in late Roman Empire architecture, a space with a trefoiled arch with three lobes, one axial and the other two to right and left.

Triforium
A shallow passage above the nave arcade and the choir in a medieval church. The triforium is usually arcaded.

Triglyph
Blocks with vertical channels which are set at regular intervals in the frieze of the Doric Order.

Trimurti (HIN)
An image showing the deities, Brahma, Vishnu and Shiva which symbolise creation, preservation and destruction.

Trikutashala (HIN)
A three-celled temple or a triple shrine.

Triratha (HIN)
The tower of a temple with three projecting rathas.

Trumeau
Describes the pier between two openings or, in Gothic architecture, the pier dividing a large portal in two parts.

Tsuridono (JAP)
A small open pavilion set over a garden pond in a shinden style estate and used as a place for aesthetic diversion.

Tudor
Describes English Late Gothic architecture between 1485–1558.

Tufa
Building stone that originates from volcano or other source and is rough or cellular in texture.

Tumulus (ISL)
The marking of a tomb with artificial earth or stone.

Turrets
Especially seen in Medieaval architecture, a small tower that often contains stairs.

Tuscan Order
Very similar to the Doric order except for its very plain entablature. The shaft is properly unfluted.

Tympanum
The triangular space bounded by the sloping and horizontal cornices of a classical pediment.

Undercroft
In medieval architecture, a chamber partly or completely underground. In a house or castle it would have been used for storage while in a church it was the crypt.

Vault
Essentially an arched ceiling (which may or may not support a floor above) constructed of stones that when stressed against each other create stability.

Vaulting Bay
A square or rectangular area that is bounded by piers or columns and covered by a ribbed or groined vault.

Vaulting boss
An ornamental feature set at intervals in a ribbed vault to hide the junctions between one rib and another.

Vault springing
The point at which the vault ribs spring upwards from the capital, corbel, or arch impost.

Vedika (HIN)
A low wall or a post-and-rail type stone balustrade that surrounds a temple.

Vernacular
'Ordinary' architecture without pretensions to grandeur. Using local materials in traditional ways, vernacular 'architecture' includes farm buildings, factories, cottages, and other simple houses. Sometimes described as "architecture without architects."

Vesara (HIN)
Architectural style between Dravidian and Nagara styles.

Vihara (HIN)
Word for Buddhist monastery.

Volute
A scroll or spiral occurring in Ionic, Corinthian and Composite capitals.

Voussoir
The wedge-shaped stones that make up an arch.

Watadono (JAP)
The corridors connecting the Shinden and tainoya in Shinden-style architecture.

Ziggurat
An important element in ancient Mesopotamian temple complexes, these high pyramidial staged tower had angles oriented to the cardinal points.

Ziyada (ISL)
The outer courtyard that surrounds a mosque and separates it from the outside world.

Turrets

THOSE THAT GOT AWAY: VISIONARY & UNBUILT ARCHITECTURE

Drawings of unbuilt, structures and destroyed buildings known only from drawings have played an important role in the history of architecture. When Frank Lloyd Wright prepared the first major publication of his work issued in 1910, it is significant that he chose not to include any photographs. Each project, built or unbuilt was represented by specially prepared, extraordinarily beautiful drawings. Wright understood the impact the drawings would have, giving equal weight to his built and unbuilt projects.

Before photography and easy travel, published volumes of drawings were the method by which architectural knowledge was transmitted. In the Middle Ages this knowledge was carefully guarded by the guilds. The Renaissance revived classical architecture and reprinted the oldest surviving text on the subject, the *Ten Books on Architecture* written by Marcus Vitruvius Pollio (first century BC) making knowledge of architecture available to a larger audience. Various editions of Vitruvius, over the years, have each had contemporary illustrations added to the text. The most famous of these is probably the edition illustrated by Andrea Palladio (1556). Palladio, whose Villa Capra near Vicenza is perhaps the most copied house ever built, issued his own theoretical treatise on architecture, his *Four Books of Architecture* (1570). This he illustrated with woodcuts of ancient buildings as well as both built and unbuilt buildings of his own design.

Architecture that has been considered visionary goes beyond what exists and often beyond what is buildable in its time. The first visionary architectural projects were the designs for ideal cities produced during the Renaissance. These design proposals predate the first appearance of utopias in literature (Sir Thomas Moore, *Utopia,* 1516), by nearly 100 years. These cities equated the *good life* with the perfection of geometric form. In his plan for the ideal city of Sforzinda (1460), the Italian architect, Filarete, designed not only the city but also its principal buildings. Designing the city as well as its buildings began a tradition that has continued into the 20th century with Tony Garnier's *Cité Industrielle* (1917), Le Corbusier's *Ville Contemporaine* (1922), and *Ville Radiuse* (1933), and Frank Lloyd Wright's design for Broadacre City (1934), a visionary proposal that prefigured the contemporary American suburb. In the 1960s the English group Archigram proposed futurist images of buildings and great mechanized cities that could walk across the landscape, float on water and hover above the earth. Among the most arresting unbuilt images of the modern city and its buildings were those created by the Italian Futurist architect Antonio Saint'Elia (1888–1916) and the American architect and illustrator Hugh Ferris, in his book *The Metropolis of Tomorrow,* 1929. On film, memorable images of the city of the future abound: Fritz Lang's *Metropolis* (1926), Ridley Scott's *Blade Runner* (1982), and architect Anton Furst's Gotham city designed for Tim Burton's *Batman* (1989).

The term *visionary architecture* was

Cita Nuova

probably first used to describe the unbuilt work of the French architects, Boulée (1728–99), Ledoux (1736–1806), and LeQueu (1757–1825). Boulée's project for a cenotaph for Sir Isaac Newton and his unbuilt design for the expansion of the Bibliotèque National in Paris (1790), are among the most powerful architectural images ever produced. In the library project the tiers of books form a visual foundation for a colonnaded Roman Forum with groups of people in the central space discussing the great ideas of the world. Like the work of Boulée, Piranesi's fanciful

Boulee cenotaph

etchings of Carceri (Prisons, 1750s) and the set designs of Giuseppe Bibiena (1740s) draw their power from their manipulation of scale and the suggestion of infinitely deep perspective space. In the 20th century, visionary architecture has been largely the province of the Futurists and Expressionists such as Hermann Finsterlin, Hans Poelzig, Bruno Taut, Erich Mendelsohn, and Frederick Kiesler.

Although more common in Europe than America, the tradition of awarding commissions for public buildings by architectural competition, has produced important and influential unbuilt architectural projects for more than two centuries. Fredrich Gilly's unbuilt design (1797) for a monument to Fredrick the Great had an enormous influence not only on Schinkel and 19th century German architecture, but on the development of European neo-classicism. Significant 20th century design competitions included the

Saarinen Tribune Tower

1922 Chicago Tribune newspaper's competition for the design of a new skyscraper office tower for their headquarters. The unbuilt entries by Eliel Saarinen and Walter Gropius along with Mies van der Rohe's contemporaneous designs for a glass skyscraper for Friedrichstrasse, Berlin (1919) and for a concrete office building (1922) influenced the design of skyscrapers and commercial structures for the next 50 years. Le Corbusier's unbuilt entries to the League of Nations (1927–8) and Palace of the Soviets (1931) competitions had an equally important influence on the development of 20th century modernism.

Like the one that got away, many architects' most significant works have often remained unbuilt or were intended as purely visionary statements of what could be. It is a curiosity that in a field as concrete as architecture, conceptual and theoretical works have often taken on, as ideas, greater importance than realized works. Perhaps it is only in a theoretical project that an uncompromised distillation of an architectural idea can be explored.

Stuart Cohen FAIA
Professor Emeritus, University of Illinois, Chicago

FROM PYRAMID TO PYRAMID A SNAP-SHOT HISTORY OF ARCHITECTURE

c.2778BC *Step pyramid of Zoser*, EGYPT.

c.1304BC *The temple of Abu Simbel*, EGYPT.

c.447BC *The Parthenon*, ATHENS.

c.221BC *Great Wall of China*.

AD70 *Colosseum*, ROME.

AD569 *Temple of the Magician*, MEXICO.

1040 *St Mark's*, VENICE.

1194 *Chartres Cathedral*, FRANCE.

1362 *Alhambra*, SPAIN.

1519 *Château de Chambord*, FRANCE.

1631 *Taj Mahal*, INDIA.

1669 *Palace of Versailles*, FRANCE.

1769 *Monticello*, USA.

1889 *Eiffel Tower*, PARIS.

1929 *Empire State Building*, NEW YORK.

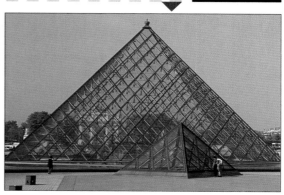

1989 *Louvre Pyramid*, PARIS.

ILLUSTRATION CREDITS

FC = front concertina
BC = back concertina

Doreen Yarwood (*with permission of B.T. Batsford Ltd*). FC2: Mesolithic hut, Etruscan tumulus; FC4: Brixworth church, S. Vitale, Gallarus Oratory, S. Sophia. FC5: S. Maria de Naranco, Little Metropole Cathedral, Trier Cathedral, Tournai Cathedral, St-Etienne, St Mark's. F6: S. Maria Laach, S. Zeno, Palazzo Loredan, Borgund Stave church. FC7:Halles Bruges, S. Millan, Siena Cathedral, Palazzo Pubblico Siena, Sor Fron, Toledo Cathedral. FC8: Ospidale degli Innocenti, Iroquois Longhouse, Cathedral of the Annunciation. FC9: Alcalà de Henares, Little Moreton Hall, Cour Carrée Louvre, Longleat. FC10: Butchers' Hall. FC11: Mauritshuis, Fredricksborg, Val-de-Grâce. FC12: Bom Jesus, Blenheim, Melk Abbey, Castle Howard. FC13: Santiago de Compostella, Royal Palace Madrid. FC14: Park Crescent, Altes Museum, Crystal Palace, Vittorio Veneto. FC15: Museum of Natural History, New Scotland Yard. FC16: Fagus Factory, Schröder house. BC1: Palazzetto dello Sport. Bridges: Alcantara, Segovia. Fortifications: Porte S. André. Introduction: Pantheon, S. Sophia, St Mark's, Notre Dame la Grande, St Martin, Amiens Cathedral, Cologne Cathedral, Doge's Palace, Burgos, Santa Maria Novella, Palazzo Rucellai, Il Tempietto, St Peter's, Fontainebleau, Seville Town Hall, Vaux-le-Vicomte, St Paul's, Zwinger, Bibliothèque National, Crystal Palace, Unité d'Habitation, S. Maria la Blanca. Glossary: all illustrations.

Sue Rose. FC2: Idlib house, Ma'dan house, Ziggurat of Ur, Ishtar Gate. FC3: Yurt, House of the Vetii, Celtic hut, Great Stupa, Fale tele, Ruma Gorga, Petra, Hadrian's Villa. FC4: Elephanta, Sung Yüeh, Temple of the Magician, Temple of the Sun, Shore Temple, Wild Goose Pagoda, Temple II, Kailasa. FC5: Kairoan, Lingareja, Susah, Enemy Observation Pagoda, Rajarani. FC6: Masid-i-Jami, Kutubiyya. FC7: San Giminiano, Cliff Palace, Ibn Tulun. FC8: Mansura, Little Hall Lavenham, Dogon house. FC9: Chambord, Gopurums, P'ai lou. FC10: Raja Birbal house, Matsumoto Castle, Villa Aldobrandini, Queen's House. FC11: Rinshunkaku. FC12:

Rinshunkaku *by Sue Rose*

Groot Constantia, Annamese houses. FC13: Chiswick House, Mount Vernon. FC14: Petrovsky Palace, Turkonoan house. BC1: Ronchamp. BC2: Hong Kong & Shanghai Bank, Bank of China. Skyscrapers: Petronas Towers, Bank of China. Fortifications: Ishtar, Matsumoto Castle, A-Z Architects: Brighton Pavilion.

Doric order *by Doreen Yarwood*

Mike Rose. FC2: Ziggurat of Ur. FC6: Krak des Chevaliers.

Automobile Association Library (UK). FC2: Newgrange, Karnak, Knossos. FC3: Epidaurus, Pont-du-Gard. FC4: S. Maria Maggiore, Great Mosque Cordoba, Dome of the Rock. FC6: Durham Cathedral, La Giralda, Bourges Cathedral. FC7: Burgos Cathedral, Caernarvon Castle. FC8: Alhambra, Frauenkirche. FC9: Villa Capra, Escorial. FC11: Palais Royal, S. Maria della Salute, Red Fort, Versailles, Invalides. FC12: Belvedere. FC14: Schauspielhaus, Paris Opera. FC15: Sagrada Familia. FC16: Casa Milá. BC2: Louvre Pyramid. Introduction: Dome of the Rock. Skyscrapers: World Trade Center. Bridges: Ironbridge, Forth Bridge. Fortifications: Harlech, Caernarvon, Conway.

Balthazar Korab. BC1: Swiss Student Center, Johnson & Co HQ, UN Secretariat, Crown Hall. BC2: Guggenheim Museum, National Gallery Berlin, Kimbell Art Gallery, Dulles Airport, John Deere HQ, East Wing Washington Gallery of Art, Salk Institute. Introduction: National Gallery Berlin, Pazzi Chapel, Salk Institute.

Jeffrey Howe. FC13: King's Chapel, Monticello. FC15: Monadnock, Guaranty Building. FC16: Woolworth Building, Bauhaus. BC1: Fallingwater, Gropius house. Fortifications: Carcassonne, Gravensteen, Pierrefonds. Skyscrapers: Woolworth Building, Tribune Tower, Sears Tower.

Chicago Historical Society/Hedrich Blessing. FC16: Unity Temple, Robie house. FC17: Tugendhat house, Farnsworth house. Mies van der Rohe: Barcelona Pavilion.

Library of Congress. FC15: Auditorium Building, Carson, Pirie, Scott. Introduction: Bayard Building.

Sydney Robinson. FC17: Jacob's house.

Louis I. Rocah. FC16: PSFS Building. BC1: Rusakov Workers' Club.

©**Dennis Finnin/AMNH.** FC18: Rose Center.

Roy Flam/Peter Dodge. BC2: Cary House.

Michael Stephenson. FC14: Houses of Parliament. FC15: Law Courts. FC16: Empire State, Flatiron. BC1: Seagram Bulding. BC2: Lloyds Building. Introduction: Houses of Parliament. Skyscrapers: Chrysler, Seagram, Flatiron, Empire State. Bridges: Brooklyn, Tower Bridge.

Cadmium. FC2: Cheops Pyramids, Abu Simbel, Stonehenge, Parthenon. FC3: Great Wall of China, Colosseum, Pantheon. FC4: Yaxchilán, Borobudar. FC5: Chichén Itzá, Mont-St-Michel. FC6: Tower of London, Angkor Wat, Notre Dame, Chartres, Campanile Pisa. FC7: Salisbury Cathedral, Winchester Cathedral, Milan Cathedral, Tulum, Forbidden City, Duomo Florence. FC9: Machu Picchu, St Peter's, St Basil's. FC10: Mexico City Cathedral, S. Giorgio Maggiore, Shwe Dagon, Sultan Ahmed Mosque, Zuiderkirke. FC11: Delft Town Hall, Taj Mahal. FC12: Grand Place Brussels, Schönbrunn, SS Peter & Paul. FC13: Radcliffe Camera, Peterhof, Winter Palace, Panthéon. FC14: Capitol Washington DC. FC15: GUM, Eiffel Tower. FC16: Métro. BC2: Sydney Opera, Centre Pompidou. Skyscrapers: Eiffel Tower. Bridges: Ponte Vecchio, Golden Gate. Fortifications: Great Wall of China, Tower of London, Eileen Donan, Rhodes, Bodiam, Amsterdamsche Poort, Neuschwanstein. Introduction: Pyramids, Parthenon, Colosseum, Notre Dame, Azay-le-Rideau, Piazza Navona, Panthéon, Great Wall of China, Forbidden City.

Kaye Yeo Ahn. Introduction: Humayan's Tomb.

Abraham Ahn. Introduction: Nijo Castle.

April Clark: Introduction: Red Fort.

EDITORIAL CREDITS

Professor Sydney Robinson (*biographical profile of Frank Lloyd Wright*);
Professor Stuart Cohen (*biographical profile of Le Corbusier and Those That Got Away: Visionary & Unbuilt Architecture*),
Professor Louis I. Rocah (*biographical profile of Mies van der Rohe*).

Editorial & Picture Research: Ruth Kogan, Jennifer Gray (*Columbia University New York*), Laura Stephenson, Anne de Verteuil, Allen C. Klein, Ali Bothwell, Beena Kamlani, Dr Indira Singh, Liz Allen & Chris Butler (*Automobile Association Library,UK*), Robert Medina (*Chicago Historical Society*), Michelle Clark (*Polshek Partnership*), Tim Ciconne www.orientalarchitecture.com.

Tower Bridge *by Michael Stephenson*

▲ **1906–10 Casa Milá,** BARCELONA, SPAIN. Beneath the naturalistic cliff-like facade of Gaudí's apartment block is a steel framework. The medieval-looking chimney pots (*below*) show the influence of Gothic/Moorish on Gaudí's aesthetic.

▸ **1911–13 Woolworth Building,** NEW YORK CITY, USA. . Designed by Cass Gilbert (1859–1934), the Woolworth was the tallest building in the world until 1930. Frank W. Woolworth admired the Gothic Revival style and had Gilbert reflect this in his design.

▲ **1925–26 Bauhaus,** DESSAU, GERMANY. HQ of the most radical design school of the 20th century, designed by its founder and Director, Walter Gropius (1883–1969).

c.1900 **Paris Métro station entrance.** FRANCE. Hector Guimard (1867–1942). Between 1899 and 1913 Guimard designed the Paris Métro station entrances in high Art Nouveau style, with prefabricated modular construction and entwining metal decoration.

▾ **1911 Fagus factory,** ALFELD-AN-DER-LEINE, GERMANY. Walter Gropius's first, and perhaps most important, building proclaimed the advent of a new kind of architecture.

▸ **1928–31 Villa Savoye,** POISSY, FRANCE. Architect: Le Corbusier (1887–1965). The signature notes of Le Corbusier's modernism are the *pilotis* (concrete supporting piles), interlinked interior and exterior spaces, and the uncompromising lines.

1902 **Flatiron Building,** NEW YORK CITY, USA. Designed by D.H.Burnham & Co, the Flatiron (named after the triangular shape of an old smoothing-iron) was the first building in New York to be supported by a steel skeleton.

▾ **1909 Robie House,** CHICAGO, USA. This Frank Lloyd Wright house has been called "one of the most influential designs in the history of architecture." Horizontal planes and multiple interior levels are Lloyd Wright trademarks.

▸ **1919–47 Hearst Castle,** SAN SIMEON, CALIFORNIA, USA. A fairytale fantasy designed by Julia Morgan (1872–1957), one of the few women to ever succeed in the profession, for the publishing magnate William Randolph Hearst.

▸ **1928–30 Chrysler Building,** NEW YORK CITY, USA. The architect William van Alen (1882–1954) beat out 40 Wall Street, New York City, as the highest building in the world by bolting on the famous Art Deco spire at the last moment.

▾ **1929–31 Empire State Building,** NEW YORK CITY, USA. The Empire State rose at the amazing rate of over two stories a week and was finished in less than the scheduled time and under budget.

1904–6 **Unity Temple,** OAK PARK, ILLINOIS, USA. Described as the "world's first modern church", architect Frank Lloyd Wright (1869–1959) rejected historical styles in favor of a masterful interplay of spaces.

▾ **1910 Steiner House,** VIENNA, AUSTRIA. Adolf Loos (1870–1933) reacted against the heavily decorative Jugendstil (Art Nouveau) and countered with an architecture pared down to unadorned essentials.

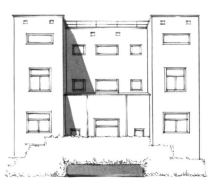

▲ **1924 Schröder House,** UTRECHT, HOLLAND. Gerrit Thomas Rietveld (1888–1964) was a member of the De Stijl movement and shared with his contemporary Le Corbusier a taste for flat roofs and uncompromising cubes.

▲ **1929 PSFS Building,** PHILADELPHIA, USA. Architect: Howe & Lescaze. The first truly modern and distinctively 20th century skyscraper in America.

---

900 – ESCALATOR RISES. The Otis Elevator Co. of New York exhibit the first escalator at the Paris Exposition.

1908 – THE MODEL T FORD INTRODUCED. The first truly mass-produced automobile rolls out of Henry Ford's Detroit factory.

1913 – A LA RESERCHE DU TEMPS PERDU PUBLISHED. By Marcel Proust, the first of seven books in his novel sequence.

1914 – WORLD WAR I BEGINS.

1905-1930 – EXPRESSIONISM IN ART TAKES HOLD. The Expressionist movement reacts against naturalism and finds new ways to visually convey the depths of human emotion and experience.

1917 – THE BOLSHEVIK REVOLUTION IN RUSSIA. By ousting the Government the Bolsheviks usher in 60 years of Communist rule.

1917 – USA DECLARES WAR ON GERMANY.

1919 – TREATY OF VERSAILLES IS SIGNED. Germany is stripped of much of its industrial and military resources following the Allied victory in World War I.

FRENCH SAILOR

1921 – CHINESE COMMUNIST PARTY FOUNDED. Mao Zedong becomes the leader of the new nation.

1925 – FIRST MOTEL. Hamilton Hotels open The Motel Inn, San Luis Obispo, California, USA.

A FLAPPER

1928 – FIRST AIR-CONDITIONED OFFICE BUILDING. The Milam Building, San Antonio, Texas, USA.

1929 – ERNEST HEMINGWAY publishes *A Farewell to Arms*, and William Faulkner *The Sound and the Fury*.

1929 – THE STOCK MARKET CRASH. The New York Stock Exchange collapses, triggering the Great Depression that grips the United States and spreads around the world.

CONTINUED ON BACK ➡

▲ **1929 Rusakov Worker's Club,** MOSCOW, RUSSIA. One of the few buildings of the Soviet avant-garde to get off the drawing board. Architect Konstantin Melnikov (1890–1974) made this proletarian cultural center an innovative expression of Russian Expressionism.

▲ **1930 Tugendhat House,** BRNO, CZECHOSLOVAKIA. Mies van der Rohe (1886–1969). The spatial concepts of Mies's earlier Barcelona Pavilion, were applied to a family house where retractable windows allowed interior and exterior to merge.

▲ **1932–36 Casa del Fascio,** COMO, ITALY. Under Fascism architecture was meant to discard 'bourgeois' decorative baggage. Giuseppe Terragni (1904–43) created this local Fascist HQ as a perfect example of Italian Rationalism.

▲ **1932 Swiss Student Center,** PARIS, FRANCE. Le Corbusier's light steel cage was perched on an elevated concrete base.

▲ **1936 'Fallingwater',** MILL RUN, PENNSYLVANIA, USA. Frank Lloyd Wright's most famous building and an icon of modern architecture. The relationship between building and landscape seems to echo Japanese traditions.

◄ **1936 S.C. Johnson & Son HQ**, RACINE, ILLINOIS, USA. Frank Lloyd Wright's forest of concrete mushrooms support a ceiling of illuminated glass that fills the workspace with light.

▲ **1938 Gropius House,** LINCOLN, MASSACHUSETTS, USA. Walter Gropius's own home has all the touchstones of Bauhaus modernism: flat roof and geometric planes, ribbon windows and, above all, no ornamentation.

▲ **1944 Jacob's House,** MADISON, WISCONSIN, USA. One of a series of Frank Lloyd Wright buildings in his 'Usonian' phase: modernist houses for the middle class.

▲ **1945–51 Farnsworth House,** PLANO, USA. Architect: Mies van der Rohe. It seems to float effortlessly above the ground, a testament to Mies's concern for the relationship between site and building.

◄ **1946–52 Unité d'Habitation,** MARSEILLES, FRANCE. Le Corbusier called his futuristic solution to housing a large number of people economically "a machine for living".

▲ **1952 Lever House,** NEW YORK CITY, USA. Architects: Skidmore, Owings & Merrill. Until 1952 Park Avenue, New York, was a barren canyon of brick, then came Lever House and its glass curtain-wall that created a revolution in commercial architecture.

▶ **1947–50 UN Secretariat,** NEW YORK CITY, USA. . The design committee included, among others, Le Corbusier and the Brazilian Oscar Niemeyer. The bold slab form is set in counterpoint to the sinuous General Assembly building below it.

▼ **1950–55 Pilgrimage Chapel,** RONCHAMP, FRANCE. A building unlike anything else in Le Corbusier's architectural output. Some critic saw it as the greatest piece of sculpture i the 20th century.

▲ **1950–56 S.R. Crown Hall, Illinois Institute of Technology,** CHICAGO, USA. Mies van der Rohe car to the IIT in 1938 and was commissioned to design a new campus, of which Crown Hall is considered the outstanding building.

▲ **1958 Seagram Building,** NEW YORK CITY, USA. Architect: Mies van der Rohe. "The lesson of the Master" an exercise in enriching the urban environment with bronze, amber-tinted glass, elegant proportions, an a generous open plaza.

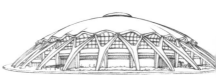

▲ **1958–9 Palazzetto dello Sport,** ROME, ITALY. Pier Luigi Nervi (1891–1979) was an Italian civil engineer and one of the 20th century's preeminent architects working in reinforced concrete.

1931 – JAPAN INVADES MANCHURIA. Japan continues its expansion into China through the decade, but the Soviet army stops their westward movement in 1939.

1933 – ADOLF HITLER DECLARED CHANCELLOR OF GERMANY.

1933 – FRANKLIN D. ROOSEVELT ELECTED 32ND PRESIDENT OF THE USA.

1933 – WOMEN'S RIGHTS. Treaty on equal rights for women is signed by 11 nations.

1941 – JAPAN ATTACKS US. Japanese warplanes attack the US fleet at Pearl Harbor. US declares war.

1944 – D-DAY LANDINGS. On 6 June American, British and Canadian forces storm Nazi-held Europe.

1939 – WORLD WAR II BEGINS IN EUROPE.

1947 – INDIA AND PAKISTAN INDEPENDENT. The once-British colony separates into India and Pakistan.

1948 – STATE OF ISRAEL DECLARED. Chaim Weizman is first president of the new state.

1949 – PEOPLE'S REPUBLIC OF CHINA DECLARED. Mao Zedong becomes first chairman of People's Central Council.

1952 – ELIZABETH II becomes queen of England.

1953 – ELVIS PRESLEY MAKES HIS FIRST PRIVATE RECORDINGS.

1955 – BILL HALEY & THE COMETS MAKE "ROCK AROUND THE CLOCK".

1957 – FIRST MAN IN SPACE. Yuri Gagarin of the Soviet Union orbits the Earth in Vostock.

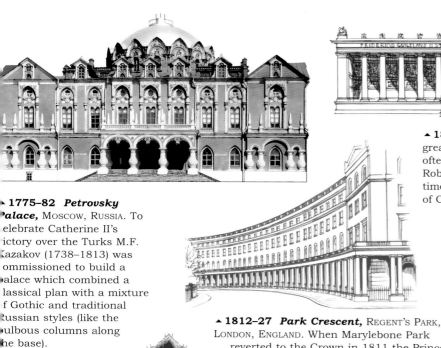

▲ 1775–82 *Petrovsky Palace,* MOSCOW, RUSSIA. To celebrate Catherine II's victory over the Turks M.F. Kazakov (1738–1813) was commissioned to build a palace which combined a classical plan with a mixture of Gothic and traditional Russian styles (like the bulbous columns along the base).

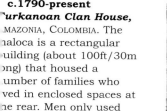

c.1790-present *Turkanoan Clan House,* AMAZONIA, COLOMBIA. The maloca is a rectangular building (about 100ft/30m long) that housed a number of families who lived in enclosed spaces at the rear. Men only used the center and front. The façade is decorated with religious symbols.

▲ 1812–27 *Park Crescent,* REGENT'S PARK, LONDON, ENGLAND. When Marylebone Park reverted to the Crown in 1811 the Prince Regent (later George IV) backed the ambitious plan by John Nash (1752–1835) to create a garden city for the wealthy in the heart of London. Present-day Regent's Park represents only a part of Nash's original plan.

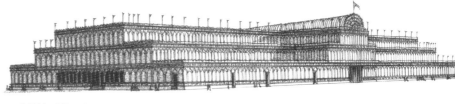

▲ 1823–30 *Altes Museum,* BERLIN, GERMANY. Another great example of Neoclassicism. Von Schinkel's design is often compared to the British Museum in London (Sir Robert Smirke 1781–1867) and built almost at the same time. The Altes Museum is superior in its bold handling of Classical forms and the execution of its detailing.

▶ 1836–65 *Houses of Parliament,* LONDON, ENGLAND. Much of the original medieval Palace of Westminster burnt down in 1834. Ninety-six architects submitted plans for a replacement building and Sir Charles Barry (1795–1860) won the competition with his elegantly simple Perpendicular Gothic design that blended sympathetically with the nearby medieval Westminster Abbey and St Margaret's Church.

▲ 1851 *The Crystal Palace,* LONDON, ENGLAND. Sir Joseph Paxton (1803–65) had designed the great greenhouse at Chatsworth House and used this skill to win a competition for a building to house the Great Exhibition of 1851. The rules of the competition stated that the building must be able to be dismantled and re-erected on another site. Paxton's solution, an iron and glass structure, was to have a profound influence on later building techniques and styles.

▲ 1818 *Piazza Vittorio Veneto,* TURIN, ITALY. Turin, close to France, had always felt its neighbor's architectural influence. The Piazza, designed by Giuseppe Frizzi and Carlo Promis, reflects that proximity in its great squares and arcaded streets.

◀ 1793–1867 *The Capitol,* WASHINGTON DC, USA. The first building was designed by William Thornton (1759–1828), an amateur architect from England much influenced by Palladio. During the War of 1812 the British badly damaged the building and it was restored first by Benjamin Latrobe (1764–1820) and then Thomas Ustick Walter (1804–88) who designed the flanking wings and central rotunda.

◀ 1819–21 *Schauspielhaus,* BERLIN, GERMANY. Designed by Karl Friedrich von Schinkel (1781–1841) in a very boldly stated Neoclassic style (*see also his Altes Musem, 1823*)

▲ 1862–75 *Opera House,* PARIS, FRANCE. A then-unknown architect, Charles Garnier (1825–98), won the competition (beating 170 other contestants) to create an opera house on a site recently cleared during Baron Haussmann's restructuring of the city. The building has a flashy nouveau-riche exuberance perfectly in keeping with the spirit of Napoleon III's Second Empire.

1776 – THE DECLARATION OF INDEPENDENCE IS SIGNED. America formally declares its intention to free itself from British control. In 1783, after the Revolutionary War, Britain finally recognizes the colonies' independence.

1789 – THE FRENCH REVOLUTION BEGINS. In 1789, the monarchy is overthrown and France becomes a republic.

1793-1794 – THE REIGN OF TERROR. Maximilien Robespierre, leader of the French revolutionary government, sends thousands to be executed by guillotine for suspected treason.

FRENCH LADY

1799 – NAPOLEON BECOMES DICTATOR OF FRANCE. Napoleon attempts to capture all of Europe, and nearly succeeds, until he is defeated at the Battle of Waterloo in 1815.

1800 – THE INDUSTRIAL REVOLUTION IS UNDERWAY. The shift from agriculture to industry begins in Britain in the late 18th century. It spreads to continental Europe and North America throughout the 19th century.

1803 – THE FIRST STEAM LOCOMOTIVE IS BUILT. Rail transportation takes a giant leap forward.

1848 – THE COMMUNIST MANIFESTO PUBLISHED. Marx and Engels are the authors of the revolutionary work that proposes a classless society run by the working common people.

1860s – PASTEURIZATION prevents infection of food. Louis Pasteur proves that food spoils from exposure to bacteria. He devises the pasteurization process to protect food from contamination.

1869-1876 – RICHARD WAGNER COMPOSES THE RING OF THE NIBELUNGS. The cycle of operas is written at the height of the Romantic movement in music.

1876 – ALEXANDER GRAHAM BELL INVENTS THE TELEPHONE.

1879 – THOMAS EDISON INVENTS THE ELECTRIC LIGHT BULB. Edison's bulb burned for 40 hours continuously.

Skyscrapers

The force and power of altitude must be in it, the glory and the pride of exaltation must be in it. It must be every inch a proud and soaring thing, rising in sheer exaltation...

American skyscraper pioneer, Louis Sullivan, 1896.

Eiffel Tower, Paris, France, 1889.
(above and right) Engineer Gustave Eiffel's colossal edifice was built for the Paris Exposition. Gigantic it was but beloved it certainly was not at first. A "truly tragic street lamp" (even Eiffel referred to it as France's tallest flag pole) and an "odious column of bolted metal" were some of the comments of early detractors. It was the tallest structure in the world for 40 years, until the Chrysler Building topped it in 1930.

From the tower of Babel to the Petronas Towers in Kuala Lumpur, building ever skyward has been a persistent theme in both lore as well as the actual history of architecture. Taller and taller buildings have evolved from practical considerations, to be sure – especially limitations of space – but colossal buildings, soaring higher and higher, carry a powerful symbolism that has been as much a reason for their existence as any other.

The term 'skyscraper' was coined in the 1880s in America, just after the first tall buildings appeared, mostly in Chicago and New York. While a decidedly modern art form, the skyscraper can trace its roots to ancient times. The impulse to build toward the heavens has been present in many civilizations. Egyptian pyramids, medieval towers, Gothic spires, Mayan pyramids, Chinese pagodas, although not strictly precursers of modern-era skyscrapers share the same desire to create high buildings that proclaim power and induce awe.

Steel-framed construction and great height are the primary defining features of skyscrapers. Other innovations were crucial in making them functional: elevator technology, fireproofing, central heating, electrical plumbing pumps, and the telephone to name some. The rapid growth of metropolitan centers in the late 1800s created the social impetus for high-rise buildings; technology did the rest.

The story of super-tall buildings usually begins in Chicago where the great fire of 1871 wiped out much of the city, and rebuilding began on a vast scale. The Industrial Revolution had made iron and steel viable as building materials. Chicago's Home Insurance Building (1885) was the first tall building to be supported by a steel skeleton of vertical columns and horizontal beams, although its ten stories make it diminutive for a modern skyscraper. The move away from load-bearing walls, along with the advent of elevators meant that buildings could shoot infinitely higher. And a new era of building was born.

Pioneering early skyscrapers included the Wainwright Building (St Louis, 1891) featuring Louis Sullivan's unique stylistic articulation; the Reliance Building (Chicago, 1894) with its revolutionary glass curtain wall; and the Barclay-Vesey Building (New York, 1926) which completed echewed historical motifs in both its massing and its decorative detail.

Other great early skyscrapers did use art-historical motifs. The Flatiron Building (New York, 1902) had its Beaux-Arts design; the Metropolitan Life Insurance Tower (New York, 1909) had a classical silhouette, and the Woolworth Building (New York, 1913) its glorious Gothic detailing. Whether quoting from the past or trying to break from it, all the great skyscrapers reflect their designers' efforts to find the proper aesthetic for an architectural form that was growing ever taller and was clearly here to stay.

The golden age of skyscraper construction is generally agreed to be the period that gave rise to the Chrysler Building (New

▾ **Home Insurance Building, Chicago, USA, 1885.** Considered the world's first skyscraper, this ten-story building (demolished in 1931) was the first to be supported by a steel skeleton of vertical columns and horizontal beams. Engineer William Le Baron Jenney's discovery that that thin pieces of steel could support a building triggered a revolutionary change in the way tall buildings could be constructed.

▸ **Flatiron Building, New York City, USA, 1902.**
Designed by Daniel Burnham and John Wellborn Root, the Flatiron (so named because its triangular profile looked like an old smoothing, or flat, clothes iron) is New York's oldest surviving skyscraper. Unlike Burnham's work on Chicago high-rises where he avoided historical references the Flatiron is loaded with classical detailing from its rusticated base to its corniced top.

◄ *1958–63 Dulles Airport,* VIRGINIA, USA. Architect Eero Saarinen (1910–61) declared "I think this airport is the best thing I have ever done."

◄ *1971–77 Centre National d'Art et de Culture Georges Pompidou,* PARIS, FRANCE. The 'Brutalism' of the 1960s and 1970s in which ventilation ducts, electrical conduits, stairs etc were given forefront exposure found dramatic expression in Richard Roger's and Renzo Piano's museum – "an oil refinery for modern art."

1959–73 Opera House, SYDNEY, AUSTRALIA. Danish architect [J]orn Utzon won an international competition with his elegant [a]nd witty evocation of sails, the highest of which is almost [2]00ft/60m above the natural stone deck.

▲ *1959 Solomon R. Guggenheim Museum,* NEW YORK CITY, USA. Frank Lloyd Wright's only building in Manhattan and one of the world's most distinctive architectural shapes. Wright had started working on the plan as early as 1942.

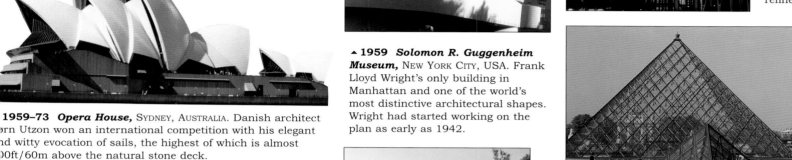

◄ *1959–65 Salk Institute,* LA JOLLA, CALIFORNIA, USA. Louis Kahn (1901–74). Research facility built for Dr Jonas Salk of polio vaccine fame. Kahn's cool and lyrical juxtaposition of buildings and site achieves an almost poetic quality.

▲ *1989 The Louvre Pyramid,* PARIS, FRANCE. I.M. Pei's glass entrance to the Louvre extension is at once regal (the pyramid as ancient symbol of royalty) yet democratically transparent.

◄ *1960 Cary House,* MILL VALLEY, CALIFORNIA, USA. Architect: Joseph Esherick (1914–98). Use of wood, light, play with space and adaptation to site made Esherick the leader of West Coast modernism.

▲ *1966 Kimbell Art Museum,* FORT WORTH, TEXAS, USA. Louis Kahn described his building as a "friendly home". The 16 barrel-vaulted roofs with their plexiglass panels bathe the works of art in indirect sunlight to create "a harmony of spaces and light."

◄ *1986 Hong Kong and Shanghai Bank,* HONG KONG, CHINA. Architect Norman Foster (with structural engineers Ove Arup & Partners) opened up the interior space by suspending floors from steel pylons.

▸ *1990 Bank of China,* HONG KONG, CHINA. I. M. Pei's fascination with the geometry of triangles (*see Louvre Pyramid and East Wing of the National Gallery of Art, Washington DC*) continued in this, one of the most elegant of skyscrapers.

1962–8 National Gallery, BERLIN, GERMANY. [A]rchitect: Mies van der Rohe. His final and [cr]owning masterpiece.

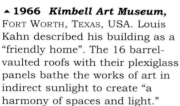

▲ *1971 East Wing, National Gallery of Art,* WASHINGTON DC, USA. Architect: I.M. Pei & Partners. A stunning complex of joined triangular buildings that create surprisingly intimate spaces for the art inside.

▼ *1999 Rose Center for Earth and Science, Natural History Museum,* NEW YORK CITY, USA. Architect: Polshek Partnership. The cube that houses the Hayden Planetarium is the largest glass curtain-wall in the USA. Its 736 panes add up to 36,000 sq. ft/3969 sq.m.

1963 Deere & Co Administrative Center, [M]OLINE, ILLINOIS, USA. Architect Eero Saarinen [th]ought his Dulles Airport (*see 1958*) one of his [fin]est achievements, while many others have [ha]iled his Deere HQ as "one of the great [A]merican mid-century buildings."

▸ *1978–86 Lloyds Building,* LONDON, ENGLAND. Richard Rogers (*see Pompidou Center, 1971*) again inverted the usual order. Those 'service' elements that had traditionally been hidden are here paraded in all their stainless steel glory.

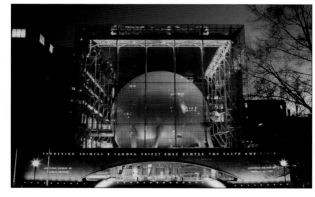

1961 – CUBAN [MI]SSILE CRISIS. [Pr]esident John [F] Kennedy [su]ccessfully [pr]essures the [So]viets to [re]move [mi]ssiles based [in] Cuba.

1963 – JOHN F KENNEDY ASSASSINATED.

1963 – THE SEXUAL REVOLUTION BEGINS. The emergence of the contraceptive pill in 1960 triggers what is later termed the "sexual revolution," a period in the USA and Europe of sexual experimentation and freedom.

1964 – THE CIVIL RIGHTS ACT IS PASSED IN THE USA. It is the culmination of a long struggle for equal rights for African-Americans.

1965 – FIRST US TROOPS ARRIVE IN VIETNAM.

1967 – FIRST HEART TRANSPLANT. By Dr Christiaan Barnard of Cape Town, South Africa.

1968 – MARTIN LUTHER KING AND BOBBY KENNEDY ASSASSINATED.

1969 – FIRST MAN ON THE MOON. 21 July Neil Armstrong steps on to the face of the Moon.

1969 – WOODSTOCK MUSIC FESTIVAL. 500,000 people congregate at Max Jasgar's farm, Woodstock, New York, USA.

1975 – SOUTH VIETNAM SURRENDERS TO THE COMMUNISTS. North Vietnam prevails, effectively ending the Vietnam War.

1980 – JOHN LENNON MURDERED.

1981 – FIRST AIDS CASES DIAGNOSED.

1983 – THE INTERNET IS CREATED.

1989 – COMMUNISM IN EUROPE CRUMBLES. Eastern Bloc countries of Europe break free from the USSR and overthrow their Communist governments.

1991 – GULF WAR. Multi-national troops expel Iraqi forces from Kuwait.

2001 – TOWERS DEMOLISHED. Twin towers of the World Trade Center, New York, destroyed by two aircraft hijacked by terrorists.

NINETEENTH CENTURY

◂ **1868–82** *Law Courts*, LONDON, ENGLAND. Architect: George Edmund Street (1824–81). In 13th century castellated Gothic, Street managed to give variety to his long facade.

◂ **1873–9** *Museum of Natural History*, LONDON, ENGLAND. Alfred Waterhouse (1830–1905) wanted to "clothe over practical necessities with such beauty as they were capable of receiving." This he achieved by cladding the iron framework in glazed terra-cotta – a perfect material in the soot-laden air of Victorian London.

▴ **1886–9** *The Auditorium Building*, CHICAGO, USA. Architects: Louis H. Sullivan (1856–1924) and Dankmar Adler (1844–1900). A powerful expression of a multi-use complex , it houses one of the finest auditoriums in the USA (Adler was an acoustics expert).

◂ **1889–91** *Monadnock Building*, CHICAGO, USA. Architects: D.H. Burnham (1846–1912) and John Wellborn Root (1850–91). The last high-rise in Chicago to have load-bearing walls. Absence of ornament makes this a milestone in the emergence of modern architecture.

▾ **1889** *GUM Department Store*, MOSCOW, RUSSIA. Within a Renaissance-inspired exterior is a network of iron and glass balconies, walkways and domes.

▸ **1875–1919** *Sacré Coeur*, PARIS, FRANCE. Designed by Paul Abadie (1812–84). Sitting atop the hill of Montmartre, Sacré Coeur echoes the Byzantine/Romanesque cathedral of S. Front, Périgueux.

▸ **1887–90** *New Scotland Yard*, LONDON, ENGLAND. Richard Norman Shaw (1831–1912) mined many styles in this highly eclectic work: corner 'tourelles' derive from French castles, the gables from the Netherlands, the door surrounds are Baroque, and over all it has a Scottish baronial feel.

◂ **1883** *Sagrada Familia*, BARCELONA, SPAIN. Antoni Gaudi (1852–1926) drew on Spanish Gothic and Islamic traditions, among others, in designing this votive church to the Holy Family. He foresaw it as the work of generations, and to this day it still has the feeling of a construction site.

▴ **1889** *Galerie des Machines*, PARIS, FRANCE. Architects: Victor Contamin (1840–93) and Charles Dutert (1845–1906). Built for the Paris Exhibition of 1889, it was one of the most important steel-and-glass buildings of its age with an unprecedented unsupported steel span of 375ft/114m. Demolished 1910.

◂ **1895–6** *Guaranty Building*, BUFFALO, NEW YORK, USA. The Guaranty demonstrates what Louis Sullivan, its architect, meant when he said "a skyscraper should be a proud and soaring thing."

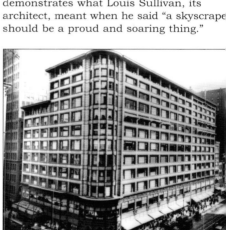

◂ **1884** *Factory Building*. NEW YORK, USA. The J. P. Hale Piano Factory is representative of the utilitarian architecture demanded by an age of expanding industrialization – "form should ever follow function".

◂ **1889** *Eiffel Tower*, PARIS, FRANCE. Although many thought it an aesthetic abomination, over two million visited it in the first year (it now receives six million a year).

▴ **1899–1904** *Carson, Pirie, Scott Store*, CHICAGO, USA. The Sullivan-designed building bears some of his trademark elements: 'Chicago' windows (a fixed pane flanked by ventilating panes), terra-cotta cladding, and exquisite cast-iron detailing

---

1880 – IMMIGRANTS POUR INTO THE UNITED STATES OF AMERICA. More than 9 million, mainly Europeans, enter the US in the last 20 years of the 19th century.

1881 – ANTHRAX VACCINE. French chemist Louis Pasteur gave the first public demonstration of his vaccine when he proved that inoculated animals were immune to the disease.

AMERICAN COWBOY

1882 – FIRST POWER PLANT. Thomas Alva Edison designs the first power station for distributing electricity.

1885 – FIRST PETROL-DRIVEN AUTOMOBILE. Karl Benz of Mannheim, Germany develops a three-wheel single-cylinder automobile.

AMERICAN TENNIS COSTUME

1886 – ALUMINUM INVENTED. American Chemist Charles Hall and French chemist Paul Herouĥ independently developed the electrolytic extraction of pure aluminum.

1887 – ELECTRIC ELEVATOR. Although elevators had existed since the 18th century, the German firm of Siemens and Halske produce the first for use in high buildings.

1890 – HENRIK IBSEN'S PLAY HEDDA GABLER FIRST PERFORMED.

1897 – BLACK GOLD. The first off-shore oil rig in operation off the coast of California.

AMERICAN BUSINESS SUIT

1898 – SPANISH-AMERICAN WAR. America invades Cuba and Puerto Rico.

1894 – FIRST PUBLIC DEMONSTRATION OF WIRELESS. Guglielmo Marconi of Bologna, Italy, in London, following the rejection of his invention in Italy.

1680

1700

1725

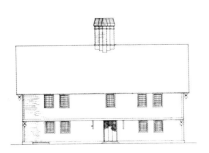

◄ **1683 *Parson Capon House,*** TOPSFIELD, MASSACHUSETTS, USA. The second story overhang and the grouped chimneys are a direct reference to the English Elizabethan houses that were the model for many early American Colonial dwellings.

◄ **1685 *Groot Constantia,*** CAPE PROVINCE, SOUTH AFRICA. Built for Simon van der Stel (1639–1712), the first Governor of the Cape Colony. Groot Constantia became a blueprint for Cape Dutch houses of wealthier landowners.

◄ **1695 *Schönbrunn Palace,*** VIENNA, AUSTRIA. Fischer von Erlach (1656–1723) became the official architect to the Imperial Court at Vienna. His original design (even more ambitious and flamboyant the final building) was finished by his son, Josef Emmanuel.

▶ **c.1700–present *Annamese floating houses,*** VIETNAM. The itinerant people of the Annam mountain lakes built their dwellings on rafts so they could be towed to different parts of the lake. Local hardwoods make them rot-resistant and the thatched roofs reduce the effects of humidity.

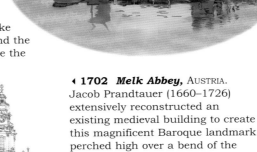

◄ **1702 *Melk Abbey,*** AUSTRIA. Jacob Prandtauer (1660–1726) extensively reconstructed an existing medieval building to create this magnificent Baroque landmark perched high over a bend of the Danube.

▼ **1705–24 *Blenheim Palace,*** OXFORDSHIRE, ENGLAND. The palace was a gift to the great soldier the Duke of Marlborough from a grateful nation. The only problem was that his formidable wife, Sarah, detested the architect, Sir John Vanbrugh (1664–1726), and banned him from the site! After Vanbrugh's death the house was completed by Nicholas Hawksmoor (1661–1736).

◄ **1690 *Grand Place,*** BRUSSELS, BELGIUM. A wonderful exuberance of Baroque, tall slender façades fitting into the small land plots of their medieval predecessors.

▼ **1699 *Castle Howard,*** YORKSHIRE, ENGLAND. The architect, Sir John Vanbrugh (1664–1726) was first a soldier and playwright before turning to architecture at the age of 35. Castle Howard was his first commission (and a stupendous undertaking for an inexperienced architect).

▲ **1723 *Bom Jesus do Monte,*** BRAGA, PORTUGAL. Like many pilgrimage churches in Portugal it is at the top of a hill reached by long flights of stairs adorned with many sculptural details – no doubt designed to make the visitor who has to climb them reflect on the redemptive nature of suffering!

▲ **1721–23 *Upper Belvedere,*** VIENNA, AUSTRIA. Architect Lucas von Hildebrandt (1668–1745) was half Austrian, half Italian and infused the building (for Prince Eugene of Savoy) with what has been described as a mixture of Teutonic discipline and Mediterranean charm.

◄ **1714–25 *Cathedral of SS Peter and Paul,*** ST PETERSBURG, RUSSIA. Built within a fortress on an Island on the river Neva, and the burial church of the czars. The architect Domenico Tressini (1670–1734) was the first important architect employed by Peter the Great.

▲ **1720 *Cape Code cottage,*** MASSACHUSETTS, USA. The Cape Cod is as sturdy as a well-made ship. Indeed, they were constructed to withstand the gales pounding in from the north-east. The rooms were clustered around a central chimney that could contain as many as four separate fireplaces.

◄ **1710–20 *Mission church,*** S. ANNA PUEBLO, NEW MEXICO, USA. The irregular outline is due to the constant erosion by wind and rain of the adobe (a type of hardened clay) construction.

1680

1700

1725

1680–1689 – THE MICROSCOPE IS PERFECTED. Dutch inventor Anton von Leeuwenhoek improves upon his earlier microscope and is the first person to study microorganisms like bactera.

1682 – FRANCE CLAIMS THE MISSISSIPPI VALLEY. Robert Cavalier, Sieur de La Salle, is the explorer who navigates the entire length of the Mississippi River and declares it the property of King Louis XIV.

1685 – THE EDICT OF NANTES IS REVOKED. Louis XIV revokes the Edict that protects the Protestants from persecution. France sanctions Catholicism only.

1685 – BACH AND HANDEL ARE BORN. Two of the greatest composers of all time are born in the same year. Both are born in Saxony, although Handel later moves to England.

1690 – CALCUTTA IS FOUNDED BY THE ENGLISH.

1694 – THE BANK OF LONDON IS ESTABLISHED.

1701 – JETHRO TULL INVENTS THE SEED DRILL. Agricultural efficiency is greatly improved by the invention of the drill plow with a seed and manure hopper.

EUROPEAN GENTLEMAN

1707 – MOUNT FUJI ERUPTS. The Japanese witness the last eruption of the great Mount Fujiyama.

1707 – ENGLAND AND SCOTLAND ARE UNITED. The Act of Union officially unites the two territories, which had shared the same monarch for 100 years.

1707 – INDIA'S MUGHAL EMPIRE EXPANDS.

1709 – FAMINE IN EUROPE. A brutal winter destroys crops and plunges Europe into famine.

1712 – ST. PETERSBURG BECOMES THE CAPITAL OF RUSSIA. Czar Peter I ("the Great") founds the city on land that was formerly held by Sweden.

▸ **World Trade Center towers, New York, USA 1972–2001.** Once the tallest buildings in the world (although they had been overtaken in 1974 by the Sears Tower in Chicago) the 'twin towers' were demolished when each was hit by a hijacked jumbo jet in a terrorist attack on 11 September 2001. All steel and aluminum, they were 1353 feet high. They were structurally innovative in that their outer cladding carried their load, quite unlike most modern skyscrapers. This actually caused the towers to remain standing much longer than might have been expected. The buildings finally collapsed from the intense heat of the jet-fuel fed fire, imploding upon themselves rather than falling over. The horrific event, killing almost 3,000 people, has forever altered the way the image of the towers is now perceived. If ever there was an example of the astonishing power of buildings as symbols, this it.

◂ **Empire State Building, New York, USA, 1931.** On its completion it broke multiple records. It became the world's tallest office building, surpassing the Chrysler by 204 feet. It was constructed in record time: its 3000 workers finished the job in only one year and 45 days. Its 2.5 million square feet of office space was greater than the Chrysler and the next largest building of the day combined. It consisted of 60,000 tons of steel, 200,000 cubic feet of Indiana limestone and granite, 10 million bricks and 730 tons of aluminum and stainless steel.

▸ **Sears Tower, Chicago, USA, 1974.** Fazlur Khan and Bruce Graham, partners in Skidmore, Owings & Merrill, were determined to break out of the plain box approach that had come to dominate skyscraper building. In fact their Sears Tower is nine skyscrapers of varying heights. Working in the highest floors can, however, be terrifying. Wind stresses have been known to shatter windows, the whole structure sways alarmingly, and the corner columns creak and groan.

> **"** If the construction of blocks of buildings ten, twelve, and even fifteen stories high is to be the rule in large cities... then insurance companies may as well prepare at once either to withdraw from these cities or double the rates of premium. **"**
>
> *The American Architect and Building News, 19 May 1883*

Comparative Heights

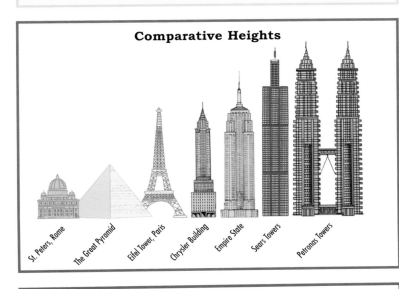

St. Peters, Rome · The Great Pyramid · Eifel Tower, Paris · Chrysler Building · Empire State · Sears Towers · Petronas Towers

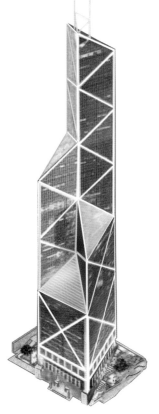

The World's Tallest Buildings

RANK	BUILDING	CITY	HEIGHT,M	FLOORS	YEAR
1	Petronas Towers	Kuala Lumpur	452	88	1998
2	Sears Tower	Chicago	442	108	1974
3	Jin Mao Tower	Shanghai		88	1998
4	CITIC Plaza	Guangzhou	391	80	1997
5	Shun Hing Square	Shenzhen	384	69	1996
6	Empire State Building	New York City	381	102	1931
7	Tuntex & Chien-Tai Tower	Kaohsing	378	85	1997
8	Central Plaza	Hong Kong	374	78	1992
9	Bank of China Tower	Hong Kong	369	72	1989
10	Emirates Office Tower	Dubai	355	54	2000

▴ **Bank of China, Hong Kong, China, 1990.** I.M. Pei's elegant and airy skyscraper upset a good many *feng shui* experts who contended that the two masts represented chopsticks over an empty bowl and that the X-braces were like the marks made against the name of a condemned prisoner. But what the building did do was to release the skyscraper from boxy predictability by offering multi-faceted angles that reward the viewer with a multiplicity of images.

▸ **Petronas Towers, Kuala Lumpur, Malaysia, 1998.** The world's tallest skyscrapers, topping the Sears Tower by 33 feet even though the antennae on the Sears is 200 feet higher than the spires of the Petronas. However, the Council on Tall Buildings counts spires and discounts antennae. Height aside, what's unique about the Petronas is their modern interpretation of an Islamic design: the floor plan is an 8-point star; the curved and pointed bays suggest temple towers. Architect Cesar Pelli's aim was to acknowldge Malaysia's past while proclaiming its modernization.

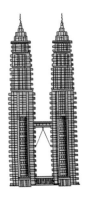

York, 1930); the Empire State Building (New York, 1931); the PSFS Building (Philadelphia, 1932); and the Rockefeller Center (New York, 1940), to name just a few. These glorious buildings shattered previous height barriers, exploited flexible materials, and gave new resonance to the concept of buildings as aspirational symbols.

Then came master architect Mies van der Rohe and the Seagram Building (New York, 1958). Mies was prominent in the Modernist movement in architecture decades before the Seagram Building was completed and the impact of the Seagram on skyscraper design was immense, and thereafter evident everywhere skyscrapers were being built. It was the prototype for the spare, glass-walled, box-shaped office building that has been the dominant form in skyscraper design over the second half of the twentieth century and into the twenty-first.

The end of the twentieth century saw a stylistic shift in skyscraper design from modernism to postmodernism, to hybrids of the two mixed with vernacular idioms. More notably it moved away from being an almost exclusively American phenomenon, to a world-wide one. Today, eight out of ten of the world's tallest buildings are in Asia.

◄ **Tribune Tower, Chicago, USA, 1925.** In 1922 the Chicago Daily Tribune held a competition to build "the most beautiful and distinguished office building in the world." Out of 300 entries (including the great modernists Eliel Saarinen and Walter Gropius) the competition was won by two unkown 'traditionalists' Raymond Hood and John Howells and their Gothic treatment, complete with flying buttresses.

▶ **The Chrysler Building, New York, USA, 1930.** The crowning jewel of Manhattan's skyline, this Art Deco masterpiece reflects the exuberance of the roaring twenties. It was completed after a ferocious race with the Bank of Manhattan to become the tallest building in the world. The Chrysler succeeded with something of a sneak attack: the stainless steel spire was assembled secretly in the fire shaft and was erected only after the competing building was finished.

▲ **Woolworth Building, New York City, USA, 1913.** Retail baron Frank W. Woolworth wanted an HQ building worthy of his fortune, even if that fortune had been made in nickels and dimes (he paid for his building in cash – $13.5 million). He chose Cass Gilbert as the architect who discovered that the verticality of the Gothic allowed him to build tall and yet still keep the building rooted in the classical tradition.

▲ **Seagram Building, New York City, USA, 1958.** Samuel Bronfman, the owner of the huge Seagram distillery empire wanted a building that would be "the crowning glory of everyone's work." His architect daughter persuaded him to employ the leading modernist of his day – Mies van der Rohe. The beautiful classical restraint of the resulting building was seen by many, including Mies, as his crowning achievement and a definitive statement of International Modernism. However, as great as the building is, it has spawned endless and mindless imitations.

1725   1750

▶ **1725 *Chiswick House,*** LONDON. Lord Burlington (1694–1753), was the most influential of the aristocratic patron/architects of the 18th century. During his two trips to Italy he was greatly influenced by Palladio, and Chiswick house owes much to Palladio's Villa Capra near Vicenza –*see 1550.*

▲ **1754–56 *Winter Palace,*** ST PETERSBURG, RUSSIA. The Empress Elizabeth commissioned Bartolommeo Rastrelli (1700–71), the leading architect working in Russia at the time, to build an immense palace on the banks of the river Neva. He was also to build her two other great palaces, at Petrodvorets and Tsarkoe Selo.

▲ **1738 *Santiago de Compostella,*** SPAIN. During the 18th century Baroque elements were often added to medieval buildings (the original cathedral at Santiago was begun in 1077). The architect of these Baroque 'improvements' was Fernando Casas y Nuova.

◀ **1747–52 *Peterhof,*** NEAR ST. PETERSBURG, RUSSIA. The original building was designed in 1716–17 by Jean-Baptiste Le Blond (1679–1719) but was then remodeled by Bartolommeo Rastrelli (1700–71) for Elizabeth, Peter the Great's daughter, who had become Empress of Russia in 1741. *See also Winter Palace 1754–56.*

◀ **1756–92 *The Panthéon,*** PARIS, FRANCE. When Louis XV fell ill in 1744 he vowed that if he recovered he would replace St. Geneviève Abbey with a grander edifice. The result is one of the great masterpieces of Neoclassicism, a return to simple, monumental symmetry: the Panthéon, designed by Germain Soufflot (1714–80).

▲ **1738–64 *The Royal Palace,*** MADRID, SPAIN. In 1734 the old fortress-like palace was destroyed by fire and the king commissioned Filippo Juvara (1678–1736) of Turin, Italy, to build a new one. Juvara died soon after work began and his plan was executed on a more modest scale by Giovanni Battista Sacchetti (1700–64).

▼ **1749–58 *King's Chapel,*** BOSTON, MASSACHUSETTS, USA. Designed by Peter Harrison (1716–75) a self-taught architect who had been born in England but emigrated to America in 1740. Built in stone and much grander than other Colonial-era churches, King's Chapel is the first in New England to depart from the tradition of church as austere meetinghouse.

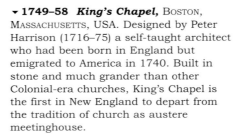

▲ **1769–1826 *Monticello,*** VIRGINIA, USA. Thomas Jefferson (1743–1826), third President of the USA, was also one of its most influential architects. He was American Minister to France 1785–89 and his travels in Europe filled him with admiration for Classicism particularly that of Palladio. Monticello was begun when he was only 24 but he continued to work on it for the rest of his life. Although a Classicist, Jefferson loved modern conveniences – he put toilets on each floor and had a wine hoist from the basement directly to the dining room!

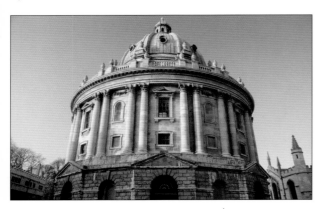

▲ **1739–49 *The Radcliffe Camera,*** OXFORD, ENGLAND. In 1714 Dr Radcliffe left provision in his will for the University of Oxford to build a library. Architect: James Gibbs (1682–1754). The cylindrical building covered with a cupola was much influenced by the buildings he had seen in Rome when he had lived there as a young man.

▶ **c. 1750 *Navaho stone Hogan,*** NEW MEXICO, USA. Hogans began as turf-built conical dwellings but by the mid-18th century had dry-stone walls and turf-covered roofs supported on a lattice of stout poles.

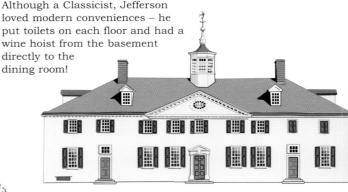

▲ **1774–86 *Mount Vernon,*** VIRGINIA, USA. The original house was built by George Washington's father in a simple 'Elizabethan medieval' style. George Washington bought the property in 1752 and added a story for his bride, Martha Custis. In 1774 he began the extensive changes we see today. This view, from the lawn side, shows the niggling disorder of the windows that disrupt the symmetry.

1725 – PETER THE GREAT DIES. He leaves Russia a major European power.

1736–1796 – EMPEROR QIANLONG RULES MANCHU CHINA. China prospers under his leadership.

DUTCH MAN

1750s – THE FACTORY SYSTEM BEGINS. England's Richard Arkwright is credited with pioneering the system that brings workers out of their homes to a communal site housing the machines for their work.

1751–1755 – THE FIRST ENCYCLOPEDIA IS PUBLISHED. Compiled by Denis Diderot and Jean d'Alembert, it attempts to summarize all of human knowledge.

1756 – WOLFGANG AMADEUS MOZART IS BORN. The great Classical composer astonishes audiences as a young boy with his musical genius. In his 35-year life, he creates many of the most beautiful and enduring works of music ever written.

1762 – JEAN-JACQUES ROUSSEAU PUBLISHES THE SOCIAL CONTRACT. It makes a strong case for the freedom of the individual against the power of the state.

1763 – THE FRENCH AND INDIAN WAR ENDS. France gives up its claim to the North American mainland, ceding to Britain all its territory east of the Mississippi, including Canada.

1764 – THE SPINNING JENNY IS INVENTED. England's James Hargreaves invents the spinning machine, vastly improving the productivity of the textile industry.

1773 – THE BOSTON TEA PARTY. Americans grow increasingly hostile toward rule by the British government. They destroy chests of tea belonging to the British East India Company.

1769 – THE STEAM-ENGINE IS PATENTED. Scotland's James Watt and Matthew Boulton use their invention to pump water out of mines.

1600

◄ **1563–1667 Cathedral,** MEXICO CITY, MEXICO. The present cathedral (which replaced a flat-roofed and primitive church built in 1525) is a fine mixture of the Baroque and Classical.

▲ **c.1600 Shwe Dagon Pagoda,** RANGOON, MYANMAR (BURMA). Built over much older foundations and added to regularly, the Shwe Dagon is inspired by Indian stupas but adds its own elegance by elongating the stubby top-knot of the Indian originals into a soaring spire.

▲ **1610–16 Sultan Ahmed Mosque,** ISTANBUL, TURKEY. Standing on a prominent site on the Hippodrome, the six-minaret mosque complements its close neighbor, the Hagia Sophia.

565 S. Giorgio Maggiore, VENICE, ITALY. One of the two of great churches built by Andrea Palladio , the other being Il entore (1577–92).

▲ **c.1600 Kojin Kyakuden** (Priest's House), ONJOJI TEMPLE, JAPAN. A typical Shoin-style house built of wood (Japan's primary building material since the start of its architectural history). This type of dwelling was used by the middle class – minor nobility, samurai chieftains, and priests.

572 'Raja Birbal's House', FATEHPUR SIKRI, AGRA, INDIA. Moghul emperor, Akbar (1556–1605), probably had this uisite red sandstone house built as part of his harem.

582 Matsumoto Castle, NAGANO, N. Also called Fakashi Castle, sumoto is one of only 12 Japanese les with a multi-story donjon, or ral fortified tower.

▲ **c.1600 Masjid-i-Shah** (Royal Mosque), ISFAHAN, IRAN. The Safavid dynasty reunited Iran in the early 16th century. Shah Abbas I (1587–1629) moved the capital to Isfahan and was responsible for planning its magnificent cityscape.

▸ **1614 Zuiderkirke,** AMSTERDAM, HOLLAND. The first church to be built in Amsterdam after the Reformation. The architect, Hendrik de Keyser (1565–1621) adopted a traditional plan but distinguished it with one of his specialties – the elegant tower. *See also Delft Town Hall, 1618.*

694 Villa Aldobrandini, SCATI, ITALY. Architect como della Porta's hillside looks down majestically the town of Frascati. The natic broken pediment, ost like book-ends in a ry, emphasizes a sical balance.

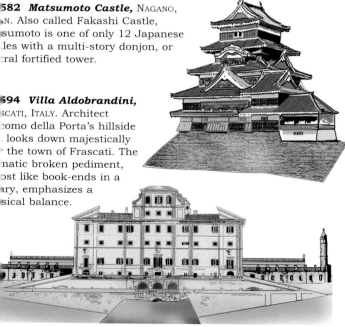

▼ **1602 The Butchers' Guild Hall,** HAARLEM, HOLLAND. Architect Lieven de Kay (1560–1627) added stone decoration to the brick buildings that predominated up until the end of the 16th century. The style, called Netherlandish Renaissance or Flemish Mannerism, was influential throughout northern Europe (*see Fredericksborg Castle, Denmark, 1642*)

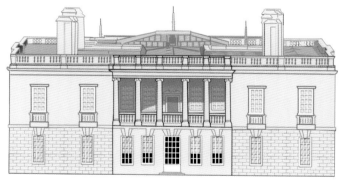

▲ **1616–35 The Queen's House,** GREENWICH, ENGLAND. Considered England's first truly Classical building. Inigo Jones (1573–1652), its architect, was a great admirer of Palladio and visited Italy to study and make detailed measurements of his buildings.

1600

Bridges

Europe, many commissioned and executed by Christian religious orders. The Gothic pointed arch was a distinguishing feature of this era, as was the multi-functional bridge, which incorporated shops, houses, chapels, towers, and other buildings into its structure. The legendary Pont D'Avignon (1187) is an example of a bridge built by a religious order, which included a chapel in its overall design.

Bridges as bustling centers of commerce, grand passageways, and/or residences sprung up during the Renaissance, exemplified by Florence's Ponte Vecchio (1345), Venice's Rialto (1591), and Paris' Pont Neuf (1607). The greatest architect of the era, Andrea Palladio (1508–1580), spawned a wave of Neoclassical bridge building through his influential books, Quattro Libri dell' Architettura. These designs were adopted primarily by English landscape designers.

Iron revolutionized bridge building. Its widespread use during the Industrial Revolution made it the material of choice for early nineteenth century engineers like Thomas Telford, Robert Stephenson, and Isambard Brunel. Iron Bridge (1779) in

The World's Longest Bridges

	Bridge	Location	Year	Feet/Meters
1.	**Akashi Kaikyo**	HYOGO, JAPAN	1998	6529/1990
2.	**Izmit Bay**	MARMARA SEA, TURKEY	UC	5472/1668
3.	**Great Belt Link**	FUNEN-ZEALAND, DENMARK	1998	5326/1624
4.	**Humber River**	HULL, ENGLAND	1981	4626/1410
5.	**Jiangyin**	YANGTZE RIVER, CHINA	1999	4543/1385
6.	**Tsing Ma**	HONG KONG, CHINA	1997	4518/1377
7.	**Verrazano Narrows**	NEW YORK, USA	1964	4260/1298
8.	**Golden Gate**	SAN FRANCISCO, USA	1937	4200/1280
9.	**Hoga KustenVeda**	SWEDEN	1997	3969/1210
10.	**Mackinac Straits**	MICHIGAN, USA	1957	3800/1158

- *All bridges are suspension bridges*
- *Length is main span length*
- *Date is year completed; UC indicates "under construction"*
- *Primary source: Bridges by Judith Dupre; updated info from www.infoplease.com*

1650

▲ **c.1650** Khaju bridge, Isfahan, built by Shah Abbas II of Persia. It is a unique combination of dam, bridge, and palace.

1750 Westminster Bridge, London. It took 500 years for a second bridge to span the Thames and relieve the severe congestion of the Old London Bridge.

▲ **1779** *(completed)* Ironbridge, Coalbrookdale, England. The first cast-iron bridge and one of the first structures to be made from prefabricated parts which cut construction time to only three months. Its single arch spans 100 feet over the Severn Gorge; its five arch ribs were each cast in two halves. The bridge was so crowded with celebrants on its 200th birthday in 1979 that parts of it actually broke off and plunged into the river. Now visitors are strictly limited to no more than 200 at any one time.

▲ **1874** James Eades' triple-arch bridge across the Mississippi river at St Louis – the world's first important steel bridge and the longest of its time.

1860

1806 Birth year of two of the greatest bridge builders in history – John Roebling of Brooklyn Bridge fame, and Isambard Kingdom Brunel of the Clifton Suspension Bridge.

1824–31 Old London Bridge replaced with a masonry bridge designed by Sir John Rennie. It was to last until 1972 when it was sold and reerected at Lake Havasu City, Arizona.

▲ **1864** *(completed)* Clifton Suspension Bridge, England. Although Brunel had built a number of wooden bridges the Clifton Suspension over the Avon Gorge at Bristol, England was his first – and last – major bridge. Work began in 1835 but repeated delays held up progress. In 1842 Brunel was told to stop work and the iron for the chain was sold. Brunel died in 1859, but the work was finished to his design by colleagues from the Institution of Civil Engineers.

1866 John Roebling built the then world-record suspension bridge over the Ohio river at Cincinnati.

1870

▲ **1879** The Tay bridge disaster, Scotland. From the very beginning of work on the Tay Bridge in 1871 there were problems, and a series of accidents cost the lives of 20 workers. In 1878 the rail service started, but at 5pm on Sunday 28th October 1879 a massive storm smashed into the bridge. A train carrying 75 passengers reached the center just as it collapsed, hurling it into the river. A Court of Inquiry blamed Sir Thomas Beach, the bridge's designer, who had completely miscalculated wind stress on the structure.

1882–89 Forth Rail Bridge, Scotland. The designers, Sir John Fowler and Benjamin Baker, attacked the problem of spanning the estuary of the Firth of Forth with the innovative use of steel and cantilevering.

▲ **1883** Brooklyn Bridge, New York City. John Roebling's brilliant design for his 1,595ft/486m suspension bridge was executed by his son, Washington Roebling, following his father's tragic death from tetanus after his foot was crushed in an accident on site.

▲ **1886–94** Tower Bridge, London. Designed jointly by the engineer John Wolf-Barry and the architect Sir Horace Jones. Tower Bridge is a 'bascule' ('see-saw' or 'rocker') bridge which allows the roadway to be raised to let ships pass beneath.

Bridges

There can be little doubt that in many ways the story of bridge building is the story of civilisation. By it, we can readily measure an important part of people's progress.

Franklin D. Roosevelt (October 18, 1931)

Bridges have always had an impact beyond their status as architectural forms or engineering marvels. They have inspired artists and poets; they have stood since primitive times as symbols of connection, of possibility, of making it to the 'other side,' even as their function remains resolutely earthy: linking point A to point B.

A bridge provides a pathway where normal surface construction is impossible or impractical. The earliest bridges were natural – fallen trees spanning gorges, huge rocks arching over streams, or vines joining tree to tree. The first man-made bridges mimicked nature's handiwork: tree trunks laid across streams; flat stones traversing shallow waterways; or vines, twisted and hung in suspension. These three types – beam, arch,

and suspension – have existed since ancient times, and remain the prototypes for even the most complex modern bridges.

The Romans were antiquity's greatest bridge builders. Roman engineering went far beyond anything previously seen, primarily through four advances: the discovery of cement; perfection of the semicircular masonry arch; development of the coffer dam; and a commitment to public works. Among the most famous of the surviving Roman bridges are the Pont du Gard (AD 14) near Nîmes, France; the Alcántara Bridge (AD 98] on the Spanish-Portuguese border; and the aqueduct at Segovia, Spain (AD 98).

Asia's history of significant bridge building predates Europe's. China was the source of many bridge forms, including the first chain-link suspension bridge, the Panho (206 BC), built during the Han Dynasty. After the decline of the Roman Empire, beam, arch, suspension and cantilever bridge building flourished in China while languishing in Europe for seven centuries. The Anji Bridge (AD 605) is far more sophisticated than anything contemporaneous in Europe.

The Medieval period saw a revival of bridge building in

2000BC

▲ **c.2000BC** Crude suspension bridges built in India and China.

c.55BC Julius Caesar spanned the river Rhine with wooden trestle bridges.

▲ **480BC** King Xerxes constructed a huge pontoon bridge across the Hellespont (the straits dividing Asia and Europe) literally and metaphorically bridging East and West.

▸ **c.AD14** The Pont-du-Gard near Nîmes, France was built by the Emperor Agrippa as part of a 21 mile/45km aqueduct to carry water across the river Gard in cement-lined channels on the top tier.

AD100

BRIDGE OVER R. TAGUS, ALCANTARA, SPAIN

AQUEDUCT AT SEGOVIA, SPAIN

▲ **c.AD100** The Roman Emperor Trajan built the great bridge at Alcántara, Spain as well as the aqueduct at Segovia.

▾ **AD605–16** An Ji bridge, Zhao Xian, Hebei Province, China. One of the most remarkable stone bridges in the world, predating anything in the West by 700 years.

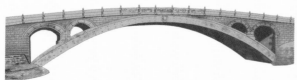

1100

1590

1187 Pont d'Avignon, France. The original length was about 3,000ft/900m and spanned the Petit-Rhône and the Grand-Rhône.

▲ **1210** Old London Bridge. Nineteen arches, none identical, created fierce tidal rips as the river Thames was forced through the narrow openings.

▾ **1345** Construction of the Ponte Vecchio, Florence, began. Attributed to Taddeo Gaddi (c.1300–66), a pupil of the great painter Giotto. The Ponte Vecchio was the first bridge in Europe to use the segmented arch (although it had been used in the An Ji bridge, China, in AD605).

1357 Charles Bridge, Prague, Czechoslovakia replaced an older stone bridge destroyed by flood in 1342. Although built by Charles IV, Holy Roman Emperor, the bridge was not named for him until 1870.

1507 Pont Notre Dame, Paris: the first stone bridge in Paris.

1591 The Rialto, Venice, designed by Antonio da Ponte (1512–97).Following a fire in 1512 that destroyed yet another in a succession of wooden bridges, Fra Giovanni Giocondo (the designer of the first stone bridge in Paris, the Pont Notre Dame) suggested a permanent stone structure. Although designs were submitted by various architects – Palladio and Michelangelo included – until the 75-year-old (and appropriately named) Antonio da Ponte daringly proposed spanning the Grand Canal with a single arch. He overcame the main problem of the soft canal bed by creating foundations made up of 6,000 alder piles packed tightly within coffer dams. The month it was completed, July 1591, it had to withstand an earthquake – which it did, triumphantly unscathed.

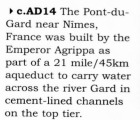

SEVENTEENTH CENTURY

▶ **1618 Delft Town Hall,** HOLLAND. Hendrik de Keyser (1565–1621) was a leading exponent of the what is called the Netherlandish Renaissance or Flemish Mannerist school which had a great influence on 17th century building styles throughout northern Europe. (*See also his Zuiderkirke, 1614.*)

▲ **1632 Le Palais-Royal,** PARIS, FRANCE. When Cardinal Richelieu became Louis XIII's First Minister in 1624 he commissioned Lemercier to build what was then known as the Cardinal's Palace. It became royal when Louis XIV left the draughty Louvre to live here. During the French Revolution is was used as a brothel. The black-and-white sculpture pillars are modern.

▲ **1631–53 Taj Mahal,** AGRA, INDIA. Once described as "a tear on the face of eternity", the Taj was built by Shah Jahan as a mausoleum to his wife Mumtaz Mahal who died giving birth to their fourteenth child. It took 20 years to build and was so expensive it cost Shah Jahan his throne.

▲ **1632 S. Maria della Salute,** VENICE, ITALY. The church is one of the glories of the Baroque and was commissioned by the city (architect: Baldassare Longhena (1598–1682) as a thanksgiving for the end of a plague epidemic. The word 'Salute' here means 'health' as well as 'salvation'.

▼ **1633 Mauritshuis,** THE HAGUE, HOLLAND. Built for Prinz Johan Maurits van Nassau by Jacob van Campen (1595–1657). The house was much copied because van Campen used the limitation of plot size to create a beautifully self-contained Classical building, still much copied.

▲ **1639–48 The Red Fort,** DELHI, INDIA. The Lal Qila (Red Fort) is a great citadel built by the creator of the Taj Mahal – Shah Jahan.

▲ **1642 Fredericksborg Castle,** DENMARK. The first Renaissance palace built in Scandinavia. The Dutch style is evident with its exuberant towers, gables, turrets, and dormers (*see the Butchers' Guild Hall, Haarlem, Holland, 1602*).

◀ **1645–67 Val-de-Grâce church,** PARIS, FRANCE. Begun by F. Mansart (1598–1666) but taken over after one year by Jacques Lemercier (c.1585–1654) who had established himself as the state architect under the patronage of Cardinal Richelieu.

▲ **1645–93 Potola Palace,** LLASA, TIBET. Founded by Ngawang Lobzang Gyatso, the fifth Dalai Lama. The White Palace went up first (1645–48) followed by the central Red Palace (1690–93). More additions were made by later Dalai Lamas, particularly in the 18th century.

▲ **1649 Interior of Rinshunkaku,** built originally at WAKAYAMA, now at YOKOHAMA, JAPAN. A fine example of the Shoin-style house that a samurai family would have lived in. This one was commissioned by a member of the Tokugawa clan, the ruling Shogunate until 1868.

◀ **1669 Palais de Versailles,** FRANCE. Louis XIV was an autocrat in every aspect of public life, particularly in architecture, and ensured that his vision was enshrined in his buildings. Louis Le Vau (1612–70) was primarily responsible for the central section. Jules Hardouin-Mansart (1646–1708) added the Galerie de Glace and the Royal Chapel.

▼ **1671–1708 Les Invalides,** PARIS, FRANCE. Designed by Libéral Bruand (1635–97) as a hospital for 4,000 disabled veterans. The dome was by Jules Hardouin-Mansart (1646–1708, see also Versailles 1669). In 1840 the body of Napoleon Bonaparte was brought back from St. Helena for interment here.

▲ **1675–1710 St Paul's Cathedral,** LONDON, ENGLAND. After the Great Fire of 1666 it was impossible to salvage the old St Paul's. Sir Christopher Wren (1632–1723) prepared two designs which were rejected before the final plan was accepted. However, durin the course of construction Wren made many modifications.

▲ **1677 Clemence Irons House,** JOHNSTON, RHODE ISLAND, USA. The extensions to the left and right are late additions. The stone chimney was originally built into the end wall. The w were clad in shingles – tile-like pieces o wood that overlapped each other.

1618-1648 – THE THIRTY YEARS' WAR. The conflict between the Protestants of Bohemia and its Catholic king spreads, ultimately involving every major European country except England. When the dust clears, France emerges as Europe's greatest power.

1611 – THE KING JAMES BIBLE. Seven years in the making, the King James Bible is published in England, retaining its currency into modern times.

1620 – PLYMOUTH COLONY IS FOUNDED IN NORTH AMERICA. Captain John Smith of the Virginia colony explores the northeastern coast and names the town of Plymouth, Massachusetts.

1642 – GALILEO GALILEI DIES. The Italian scientist is best known for inventing the microscope and building a telescope with which he makes multiple astronomical discoveries.

1643 – LOUIS XIV BECOMES KING OF FRANCE. Louis becomes king on his fifth birthday, but takes over the government in 1661. His reign of 72 years is the longest in Europe's history.

1628 – WILLIAM HARVEY HAS THE LAST WORD ON BLOOD. Modern physiology begins when Harvey publishes his treatise on the human circulatory system.

1665 – SIR ISAAC NEWTON REVOLUTIONIZES SCIENCE. Along with the law of gravity, Newton makes major scientific discoveries, including the observation that light is a mixture of different colors.

FRENCH LADY

1675 – JAN VERMEER DIES. The Dutch painter from Delft becomes the best known master of interior scenes, or "genre painting," although he is not recognized in his lifetime.

1677 – FROZEN TREATS. Ice cream becomes a popular dessert in Paris.

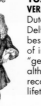

DUTCH GENTLEMAN

▸ 1390 *The Little Hall,* LAVENHAM, SUFFOLK, ENGLAND. A wood-framed house funded by the profits made from the local wool industry. A hall for eating and entertaining was at the right, while the sleeping quarters were on the upper floor on the left.

◂ c.1320 *The Great Mosque of al-Mansura,* TLEMCEN, ALGERIA. When the Maranids besieged Tlemcen in the early 14th century they turned their camp into a city and built a great mosque. All that remains now is the huge tower-like minaret.

▸ c.1400 *The Castillo,* TULUM, MEXICO. Built on a headland overlooking the azure Caribbean Sea Tulum represents the end of the great Mayan architectural tradition, with little of the sophisticated detailing found at Chichén Itzá or Uxmal.

◂ 1344 *St Vitus,* PRAGUE, CZECHOSLOVAKIA. The cathedral was designed by a Frenchman, Matthieu of Arras who died in 1352 when the east end was almost completed. The building was finished by the great architect, Peter Parler.

◂ 1360 *Winchester Cathedral,* ENGLAND. The west front (*foreground*) dates from 1360 although the transepts are much earlier (1079–93).

▸ 1419 *Ospidale degli Innocenti,* (*Foundling Hospital*) FLORENCE, ITALY. Filippo Brunelleschi (1377–1446). Brunelleschi's façade is part in 'the ancient manner' and part Romanesque.

◂ 1406– *The Forbidden City,* BEIJING, CHINA. Most of the luxurious palaces of Chinese emperors were destroyed when their reigns ended. Only the Forbidden City, built in the Ming and Qing dynasties, survives.

1387 *Milan Cathedral,* ITALY. The greatest rely Gothic building in Italy (which is explained Milan's proximity to northern Europe). Started der the Visconti dukes of Milan, the cathedral s not completed until the 19th century.

▲ 1362 *The Court of the Lions,* ALHAMBRA, GRANADA, SPAIN. The great palace complex was one of the last Moorish building enterprises in Spain (they were finally expelled in 1492). The lions surrounding the fountain are a rare example of freestanding sculpture in Islamic art.

▾ c.1450 *Iroquois longhouse,* NEW YORK STATE, USA. Constructed of poles and covered in elm bark. Built to house several families who each had sleeping bays with raised bunk-like beds off a central hallway.

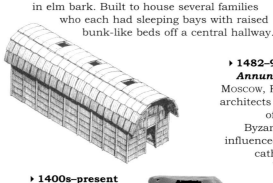

▸ 1400s–present *Dogon house,* MALI, AFRICA. The Dogon and Tellem peoples built their houses and granaries of stone and adobe. Sacred objects were placed in the niches on the façade.

▲ 1452 *Hôtel-Dieu,* BEAUNE FRANCE. Built by Cardinal Rolin, the duke of Burgundy's Chancellor, as a hospital for the poor of Beaune. Part is now a museum but it still houses a functioning hospital.

▲ 1420–36 *The Duomo,* FLORENCE, ITALY. The dome was built on to the existing medieval cathedral by Brunelleschi. In order to spread its massive weight (it is 138ft/46m in diameter) he used a double-shell construction.

▲ 1470–86 *Frauenkirche,* MUNICH, GERMANY. Typical of the large South German hall church, the Frauenkirche ('Church of the Madonna') was designed by a local architect, Jorg von Halsbach.

▸ 1482–9 *Cathedral of the Annunciation,* KREMLIN, MOSCOW, RUSSIA. Built by architects from the city of Pskov in a Byzantine style influenced by the cathedral of Vladimir.

21 – DANTE DIES. Dante hieri, author of the Divine nedy, dies at Ravenna.

337–1453 – THE UNDRED YEARS' WAR. A ries of wars between gland and France sees any English victories, but ds with French King harles VII pushing the glish back to Calais.

1347–1352 – THE BLACK DEATH. The bubonic plague kills at least a third of Europe's population. It is passed to humans by fleas that have bitten rats carrying the toxic bacteria.

1368 – MING DYNASTY IS FOUNDED. China's Ming dynasty, initially ruled by Emperor Hongwu, lasts for 300 years. The Chinese capital moves from Nanjing to Beijing in 1421. By 1600, Beijing is the largest city in the world.

1378-1417 – THE GREAT SCHISM. The establishment of an Avignon papacy in 1309 creates a rivalry between two separate papacies: Rome and Avignon. Tensions reach their peak in the period known as the Great Schism.

1381 – THE PEASANTS' REVOLT. King Richard II of England imposes a tax that triggers a peasant's rebellion, led by Wat Tyler and John Ball. The rebellion succeeds, but concessions are withdrawn when Tyler is killed by the mayor of London.

1386 – THE CANTERBURY TALES. Geoffrey Chaucer begins the acclaimed work of literature, which he left incomplete when he dies in 1400.

1430-35 – THE BRONZE DAVID. Donatello unveils his bronze statue of David, believed to be the first free-standing sculpture since ancient times.

ITALIAN ARMOR

1455 – THE GUTENBERG BIBLE. Johannes Gutenberg creates the first printing press using movable type in Germany in 1450. The Bible is printed 5 years later.

1467 – CIVIL WAR IN JAPAN. The Onin War marks a turning point leading to the decline of shoguns and the rise of daimyos, or regional military leaders. Japan's central shogunate is splintered into hundreds of separate feudal states.

Fortifications

The history of fortification is as old as the human race. A hilltop defended by a thick hedge of branches and thorns, perhaps surrounded by a ditch, may have been rudimentary, but those principles of construction, much elaborated, served castle construction for many centuries. As the nature of warfare changed, the shape, height, thickness and function of the walls also changed, but the essential principle remained the same.

For centuries military techniques altered only very gradually, and so castles remained relevant. In the 15th century, however, the advent of the cannon changed all that. Stone walls could no longer resist the mighty forces of artillery, and so the castle was transformed into something purely decorative. That is not to say that the castle died out completely. For example, the Maginot Line, a series of fortifications built by the French during the 1930s to deter attack from Germany, took the castle underground. All to no avail, however, as the German army demonstrated decisively at the beginning of World War II.

Archeology has uncovered extensive fortification throughout those areas of the earliest fixed settlements in our history: Mesopotamia, Egypt, and Greece. For example, the earliest walls of the famed city of Jericho were built c.8000 BC, while those of Babylon predate1900 BC. The strongly fortified hill towns of Mycenae and Tiryns in Greece date from c.1300 BC, and in Britain, the great earthwork fortress of Maiden Castle, Dorset, (still clearly delineated today) was constructed about 300 BC.

The Romans were expert fortifiers as well as effective besiegers. Legionaries carried with them the materials needed to construct temporary defenses wherever they camped, and as soon as they had established their rule built camps, outposts, frontier lines (the Limes Germanicus in Germany of about AD 200 and Hadrian's Wall in Britain, AD 122–25, are the most famous) and fortified cities throughout their empire (Nîmes, Autun, and Senlis in France; Colchester, York and Chester in England, have particularly good remains).

With the collapse of the Roman empire in the 4th and 5th centuries the history of fortification shifted to the Byzantine empire under continual attack on all sides. Because timber is scarce in this part of the world the Byzantines tended to build in stone, both great walled encirclements of cities (most notably Constantinople in 413) and castles. It was this tradition that the Muslims (particularly Saladin in the 12th century) adapted and from which Crusader invaders learned important lessons which they took back to Europe. For example, the great Château Gaillard in France was built by Richard I (completed 1198) following his experience during the 3rd Crusade (1189–92). The Crusaders also built massive fortifications in the Holy Land itself (combing the Muslim tower and Byzantine curtain-wall models), and the Krak des Chevaliers in Syria (begun 1150), built by the Knights Hospitaller, is one of the most spectacular and remarkably well-preserved (the principle of the double-wall defense employed at Krak was later applied to the still-impressive fortifications of the French town of Carcassonne during the 13th century).

The 11th century ushered in a massive expansion of castle building in western Europe. The Normans of France were at the forefront of new developments, and their conquest of England in 1066 initiated many new castles. One of the main types was the motte-and-bailey – essentially an elaboration of the ancient defended hill. The motte or mound (sometimes man-made) on which stood a tower, while a larger area, the bailey, also protected by a ditch-moat and earth palisade or sometimes a wall, protected the locals and their livestock. Another castle type, the rectangular stone keep, was also built throughout northern France and England (the most famous being the White Tower of the Tower of London, built 1070).

Edward I (1272–1307), king of England, undertook one of the greatest building programs in the history of the castle during his pacification of Wales. Caerphilly (1267–77), Conway (1283–87), Caernarvon (1285–1322), Harlech (1285–1290), and Beaumaris (1295-1320) still stand as his legacy.

8000BC The ancient walled city of Jericho was surrounded with a 25ft/8m wide 6ft/2m deep ditch cut from solid rock

1600BC Ashur, ancient capital of Assyria, was protected by 'curtain' walls, the connecting walls linking up towers or bastions.

▲ **c.1300BC** The Lion's Gate, Mycenae, Greece. The walled city could only be approached by one track and entered through heavily defended gateways.

▶ **600 BC** Nebuchadnezzar II's Babylon was protected by walls 23ft/8m thick, with towers and a moat.

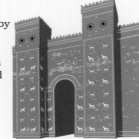

400BC Rhodes. The island fortifications, particularly the use of arches and piers, was later adopted by the Romans and Byzantines.

▲ **300BC** Maiden Castle, Dorset, England. A concentric circle earthwork hill-top defense.

▲ **c.221BC** The Great Wall of China. Almost 2,300 miles /4000km long. Much of the present wall was constructed during the Ming Dynasty, 14th–16th centuries AD.

215BC Syracuse. The first use of loopholes or muertières, at that time simple vertical slots through which archers could fire.

37BC Herod the Great constructs the great walls of Jerusalem.

30BC Herod builds the hill-top fortress of Masada, surrounding the whole of the plateau at the top with a wall 12ft/4m high and 18ft/6m thick. Like many later medieval castles it was an isolated fortress built to defend a leader and his followers. It took the Roman general Flavius Silva many months of intensive siege in AD70, including building a huge ramp which is still visible, before the citadel was captured. The Jewish defenders chose suicide over capture.

Porte St André, Autun

▲ **15BC** Roman fortified gates: For example, Porte Auguste, Nîmes; Porte St André, Autun, both in France.

4BC The first mention of the portcullis (a wood and iron gate that could be lowered and raised) by the Roman Aeneas Tacticus.

c. 200AD The *Limes Germanicus*. A series of Roman fortifications stretching 300 miles/480km from the Rhine to the Danube.

122–25AD Hadrian's Wall built to divide Roman-occupied England from Scotland. It was 73 miles/117km long, about 10ft/3.5m wide and about 20ft/7m high, with fortified camps every 4 miles/6km of which the largest and best preserved is Housesteads.

300AD Roman Porte Nigra, Trier, Germany.

▲ **413** The walls of Constantinople, punctuated every 60 yards/meters by towers.

527–565 Emperor Justinian undertook extensive castle building throughout the Byzantine empire.

▼ **Mid-11th Century** Motte-and-bailey castles. "It is the custom of the nobles of that neighbor-hood [north-east France] to make a mound of earth as high as they can and dig a ditch about it. The space on the top of the mound is enclosed by a palisade of very strong logs, strengthened at intervals by towers. Inside the enclosure is a citadel or keep. The entrance to the fortress is by means of a bridge." Jean de Colmieu, 1130.

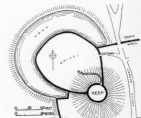

Bridges

Shropshire, England, was the first all-iron bridge and still stands as a monument to the advent of the Industrial Age. By the turn of the century, a new material was embraced that expanded even further how big, how long, and how mighty (while seeming lighter) bridges could be. Steel was the ticket. It was stronger and more flexible than iron, and made more design variations possible. New York's Brooklyn Bridge (1883), designed by John Roebling, remains one of the world's most famous steel suspension bridges. Leading bridge designers James Eads, Benjamin Baker, and Gustave Eiffel, also exploited steel to magnificent effect, making lasting contributions to the world pantheon of spectacular bridges.

The twentieth century was a Golden Age for American bridge building. The Brooklyn Bridge was followed by a series of ever-longer suspension structures: San Francisco's Golden Gate (1937), Michigan's Mackinac Straits (1957), New York's Verrazano Narrows (1964), to name a few. But Europe and Asia quickly joined in toward the end of the century, producing astonishing, groundbreaking bridges into the millennium and beyond. Denmark's Great Belt (1998), Hong Kong's Tsing Ma (1997), and Japan's Akashi Kaikyo (1998), are some of the bridges that far exceeded what was once thought possible in terms of sheer length. New materials and new forms continue to alter bridge design the world over. Prestressed concrete, joining steel in popularity in the twentieth century, is giving way to experiments with new hybrid materials. New types, like cable-stayed variations, are increasingly popular in the twenty-first century, contributing to the world landscape quite a few immensely strong but paradoxically delicate-looking structures. Avant-garde architect-engineer Santiago Calatrava's most celebrated bridge, the Puente del Alamillo (1992) in Seville, Spain, is a shining example.

Three thousand years of bridge building make it easy to understand why Roosevelt saw in it a parallel to the "story of civilisation." It's the story of human achievement, of human stumbling, of human striving. Its history, its present, and its future all speak volumes about who we are and where we are going.

1920

1927–31 George Washington Bridge, New York City. Designed by Othmar Amman and built by the Roebling Co. The second car deck was added in 1962.

1932 Sydney Harbour Bridge, Australia. Designed by English engineer Ralph Freeman, the arched cantilever bridge is the most massive of its kind in the world.

▲ **1933–37** Golden Gate Bridge, San Francisco, USA. Designed by Charles Ellis under the direction of Joseph Strauss. Its suspended span is 4,200ft/1,280m. Two hundred thousand pedestrians had the free run of the bridge on its opening day, 27 May 1937. Its grace and majesty have inspired countless artists and writers, but it also has the dubious distinction of the being the world's most popular site for suicides.

1950

1954–57 Mackinac Straights Bridge, Michigan, USA. With a suspended span of 3,800ft/1,158m, the Mackinac was second only to the Golden Gate, San Francisco, when it was built.

◀ **1940** Tacoma Narrows Bridge collapse. The catastrophic failure of the Tacoma Narrows Straights Bridge in Washington State, USA remains one of the most notorious of all time. It self-destructed on 7 November 1940 a mere four months after its opening on 1 July 1940. Before its demise it was nicknamed 'Galloping Gertie' because it swayed and rippled even under light winds. Official cause of death: fatal torsional oscillation.

1960

▲ **1966** Tagus Bridge, Lisbon, Portugal. Europe's first long-span suspension bridge. The exceptional deck height of 230ft/70m allows shipping to pass in and out of the busy port of Lisbon.

1978 New River George Bridge, West Virginia, USA. The world's longest steel arch.

1981 Humber Bridge, England. For seventeen years it held the record for the longest suspended span (4,624ft/1,410m) until superseded by Denmark's Great Belt East Bridge and Japan's Akashi Kaikyo Bridge, both completed in 1998.

1998 *(completed)* Akashi-Kaikyo Bridge, Kobe and Awaji-shima, Japan. The longest, tallest, and most expensive suspension bridge built to date. It stretches 12,828ft/4,276m and cost $4.3 billion to construct. Its two towers, at 928ft/309m are the tallest bridge towers in the world. Engineers armed the all-steel bridge to withstand the worst of Japanese hurricanes, tsunamis, and earthquakes. In fact the bridge did indeed survive the catastrophic Great Hanshin Earthquake of 1995, although when the shaking subsided it had grown three feet longer!

200? In 1998 the go-ahead was given to build the Straits of Messina Bridge, Italy. Linking the island of Sicily with mainland Calabria, it will be 10,000ft/3,300km long and able to withstand wind forces of 345mph/216kmh and earthquakes up to 7.1 Richter. It will have 12 lanes of highway capable of carrying 9,000 vehicles per hour and, in addition, there will be two railway tracks.

SIXTEENTH CENTURY

1500

1550

▼ **c.1500** *Gopurums (towers)* IN THE TIRUVANNAMALAI TEMPLE COMPLEX, TAMIL NADU, INDIA. The towers are positioned to protect the central temple, dedicated to Surya, deity of the Sun.

◄ **c.1500** *Machu Picchu*, PERU. The terraced Inca site was both a place of habitation as well as a ceremonial and religious complex. The massive granite blocks were cut so accurately that they fitted perfectly without the use of mortar (so strongly bonded that not even earthquakes have managed to dislodge them).

◄ **1506–1612** *St Peter's*, ROME, ITALY. In 1503 the newly elected Pope Julius II decided to rebuild the 1200 year old basilica that had been founded by the Emperor Constantine. Many architects were involved but two were to make the major contribution. Bramante took on the initial redesign. In 1546 Michelangelo took on the job (refusing any payment) and worked on it until his death in 1564.

▲ **1515–23** *Château de Chenonceaux*, FRANCE. At different times the home both of Diane de Poitiers, Henry II's mistress and Catherine d' Medici, his wife. The central structure was built on the foundations of a medieval water-mill. The five-arched bridge was designed by Philibert de l'Orme (c.1510–70) between 1556–59, and the upper gallery by Jean Bullant (c.1520–78) in 1576.

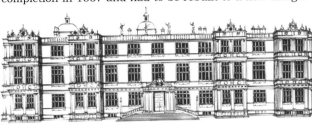

▲ **1519–47** *Château de Chambord*, FRANCE. Originally intended as a simple hunting lodge for François I, the project grew to a massive size. Domenico da Cortona created the first design, and Leonardo da Vinci may have had some involvement.

▸ **1522–66** *Five-arched p'ai lou*, BEIJING, CHINA. The commemorative arch (*p'ai lou*) is a gateway to an avenue leading to the tombs of Ming emperors. It is built of white marble with a blue-glazed tile roof.

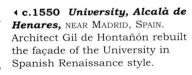

▲ **1546** *Cour Carrée*, LOUVRE, PARIS, FRANCE. The wing to the left (as we look at it) of the central building (Pavillon de l'Horloge) is by Pierre Lescot (c.1510–1578) and built between 1546–55. The Pavillon and the wing to its right are by Jacques Lemercier (1585–1684) and built 1624–54.

▲ **1550–69** *Villa Capra*, VICENZA, ITALY. Also known as the Rotonda due to the round plan of the central salon. Andrea Palladio's circle-within-the-square design became particularly popular in England – *see Chiswick House, 1725.*

◄ **c.1550** *University, Alcalá de Henares*, NEAR MADRID, SPAIN. Architect Gil de Hontañón rebuilt the façade of the University in Spanish Renaissance style.

▲ **c.1550** *Hakka houses*, FUKIEN, CHINA. The Hakka people migrated from central to southern China from the 3rd century onwards. Feeling isolated in their new environment, they built multi-story dwellings to accommodate communal living.

▼ **1550–80** *Longleat House*, WILTSHIRE, ENGLAND. Restrained Classicism makes Longleat one of the finest Elizabethan houses in England. It burned down just before completion in 1567 and had to be rebuilt to a new design.

▼ **1554–1679** *St Basil the Blessed*, MOSCOW, RUSSIA. Begun by Ivan the Terrible the cathedral church was designed by two Russian architects, Postnik and Barma. The fabulous coloring of the domes was completed in the 17th century.

▲ **1559** *Little Moreton Hall*, CHESHIRE, ENGLAND. Half-timbered houses were built for the expanding middle class who wanted ostentatious decoration without having to pa the higher prices for a similar effect in stone.

▲ **1559–84** *The Escorial*, NEAR MADRID, SPA The architect Juan de Herrera (c.1530–97) established a pure classical style to the poin of severity, which was appropriate because t Escorial was a monastery which his patron, king Philip II, a renowned ascetic, used as a religious retreat.

1500

1550

1492 – CHRISTOPHER COLUMBUS SAILS TO THE NEW WORLD. Columbus sets out for Asia, under the patronage of Ferdinand and Isabella of Spain. He lands at a Caribbean island, believing he is somewhere near Japan.

1500–1510 – TRANS-ATLANTIC SLAVE TRADE BEGINS. Europeans begin exploring the interior of Africa and establish the Atlantic slave trade.

1493 – HABSBURG MAXIMILIAN I BECOMES HOLY ROMAN EMPEROR. Strategic alliances in Germany unite the territories of the Habsburgs with those of Luxembourg and Burgundy. In German folk legend, Maximilian is known as "the last knight."

1502 – MONTEZUMA II RULES THE AZTECS. The 22-year-old is crowned emperor of the Aztecs of Mexico. He still controls the territory when the Spanish conquistador Cortes arrives in Mexico in 1519.

1501 – MICHELANGELO BEGINS WORK ON DAVID. The great Florentine master sculpts the Pietà and Bacchus, and begins work on the statue of David.

1503 – MONA LISA. Leonardo da Vinci paints the Mona Lisa, one of the most celebrated paintings of all time.

1513 – POWER OF POLITICS. Niccolo Macchiavelli writes The Prince, a brilliant commentary stemming from the struggle between royal power and the power of the nobility and churchmen.

GERMAN LADY

1517 – MARTIN LUTHER'S THESES. German monk Martin Luther nails his 95 theses, or complaints against the Catholic church, to a church door in Wittenburg. This and ensuing events touch off the Protestant Reformation.

1519–1522 – MAGELLAN CIRCLES THE WORLD. Portuguese explorer Ferdinand Magellan searches for a western route from Portugal to the Spice Islands. He manages to circumnavigate the globe.

GERMAN NOBLE

1531 – HENRY VIII ESTABLISHES THE CHURCH OF ENGLAND. King Henry's church is essentially Catholic in doctrine, but enables him to end papa authority in England. It conveniently allows him to obtain a divorce.

1547 – IVAN "THE TERRI BECOMES CZAR OF RUSSIA Ivan IV is Russia's first c

1078 The White Tower, TOWER OF LONDON, ENGLAND. The original keep, built by Bishop Gundulf, is the oldest part of the Tower of London complex.

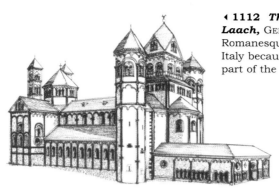

◄ **1112 The Abbey of Maria Laach,** GERMANY. German Romanesque drew much from Italy because both countries were part of the Holy Roman Empire.

▼ **1080 Masjid-i-Jami,** ISFAHAN, IRAN. The Seljuk Turks controlled most of Asia Minor by the 11th century. One of their innovations was the round minaret.

▼ **c.1120 Angkor Wat,** CAMBODIA. Influenced by Indian temple architecture, Angkor Wat is the largest religious building in the world.

◄ **c.1150 The Kutubiyya Minaret,** MARRAKESH, MOROCCO. Built by the Almohad dynasty, the minaret was originally faced with painted plaster.

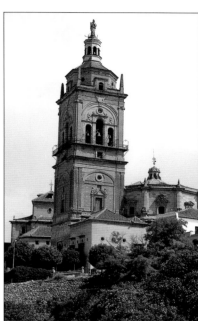

▲ **1184 The Giralda Tower,** SEVILLE CATHEDRAL, SPAIN. Seville Cathedral is the largest Gothic building in Europe and was built on the site of a mosque, the minaret of which is the Giralda Tower.

▸ **1140 Church of S. Zeno,** VERONA, ITALY. The west façade is very simple and beautifully proportioned, the porch columns supported on the backs of lions.

1093 Durham Cathedral, ENGLAND. Perched high above the river Wear, Durham is one of the greatest, perhaps the most magnificent, of all Romanesque cathedrals. Apart from the towers, it was completed in only 40 years, with every part vaulted in stone.

▲ **1144 Krak des Chevaliers,** SYRIA. The 'chevaliers' (knights) in question were the Knights Hospitaller, a crusading military/religious order that took control of the site in 1144 and defended it successfully during 11 sieges. The castle finally fell to the Sultan of Egypt in 1271.

▼ **1163–c.1330 Notre Dame,** PARIS, FRANCE. Pope Alexander III laid the first stone on a site of a Roman temple and started 170 years of intensive work by armies of Gothic architects and craftsmen. During the French Revolution much of its statuary was smashed and it was renamed the Temple of Reason, only to reopen as a cathedral in 1802.

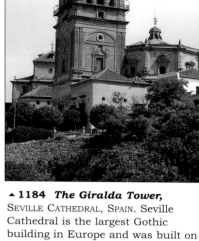

▸ **1190–1275 Bourges cathedral,** FRANCE. Interior of the nave looking toward the choir. Bourges, begun by Bishop Henri de Sully, is one of the grandest of all medieval churches. Its design was heavily influences by Notre Dame in Paris.

c.1100 Palazzo Loredan, VENICE, ITALY. Venetian Romanesque shows the strong influence of Venice's close links with Byzantium and the East.

▲ **1150 Borgund Stave church,** NORWAY. The *mast* or *stave* wooden churches of Norway are unique in Europe, although few have survived the ravages of time.

▸ **1174 The Campanile** ('Leaning Tower'), PISA, ITALY. About 100 years after the start of construction the tower began to take on its famous tilt. It wasn't until 1350 that the topmost belfry was added.

▲ **1194–1260 Chartres Cathedral,** FRANCE. Money to pay for the cathedral came from rich and poor alike. It is a city church, built for popular, rather than monastic or pilgrim, worship.

1086 – PROPERTY RIGHTS. The Domesday Book, a survey of property-holders of England, is produced.

1088 – HIGHER LEARNING. The first university is established in Bologna, Italy, evolving from the cathedral and monastery schools that preceded it.

1094 – EL CID VANQUISHES THE MOORS. The Spanish warrior Rodrigo Diaz de Vivar conquers Valencia, Spain. He is known as El Cid, meaning "chief" in Arabic.

1096–99 – THE FIRST CRUSADE. The First Crusade, led by Godfrey of Bouillon and others, captures Jerusalem.

1100 – LANGUAGE SHIFTS. Middle English supersedes Old English, and the dialect of the Ile-de-France becomes the prevailing idiom of France.

1101 – CHINA ELEVATES PAINTING. The Imperial Academy of Painting in China is founded by Chinese painter Hui Zong.

1123 – OMAR KHAYYAM DIES. The Persian poet and mathematician, most famous for his poetry series *The Rubaiyat*, was born in 1027.

EUROPEAN ARMOR

1150–1159 – COMPASSES IN CHINA. Chinese seamen and caravan leaders employ crude magnetic compasses to navigate their journeys.

1151 – CHECKMATE. The game of chess arrives in England. It is thought to have originated a century earlier in India.

1187 – SALADIN TAKES BACK JERUSALEM. The great Muslim leader Saladin becomes sultan of Egypt in 1175. He leads the force that recaptures Jerusalem from the crusaders a decade later.

1189–92 – THE THIRD CRUSADE. The Third Crusade is led by Barbarossa, Richard the Lionheart, and Philip II.

1192 – DELHI EMERGES AS POLITICAL CENTER OF INDIA. Turk and Afghan Muslims create the Sultanate of Delhi. Delhi remains the locus of Indian politics for the next 700 years.

A–Z Architects

Major architects mentioned and their principal buildings.

Brighton Pavilion, 1815–21 by John Nash 1752–1835.

Aalto, Alvar 1898–1976
- LIBRARY, Viipuri, Finland, 1927–34
- SANATORIUM, Paimio, Finland, 1928–33
- FINNISH PAVILION, Paris Exposition, 1937
- VILLA MAIREA at Noormarkku, Finland, 1937–39
- BAKER DORMITORY, Massachusetts Institute of Technology, Cambridge, Mass., 1946–49
- TOWN HALL, Säynätsalo, Finland, 1949–59
- HELSINKI UNIVERSITY OF TECHNOLOGY, Espoo, Finland 1952–57
- FINNISH NATIONAL PENSIONS INSTITUTE, Helsinki, Finland 1952–6
- CHURCH, Imatra, Finland 1956–9
- LIBRARY, St Benedict Abbey, Mt Angel, Oregon, 1964–68.

Adam, Robert (1728–92); John (1721–92); James (1732–90)
- DUMFRIES HOUSE, Edinburgh, 1750–4
- KEDDLESTON HALL, Derbyshire, 1759–70
- ADMIRALTY SCREEN, London, 1759–60
- SYON HOUSE, 1762–9
- OSTERLEY PARK, 1763–80
- LIBRARY, Kenwood House, 1767–9
- GENERAL REGISTER HOUSE, Edinburgh, begun 1774
- CULZEAN CASTLE, Scotland, 1777–92
- EDINBURGH UNIVERSITY, Edinburgh, 1789
- SETON CASTLE, Scotland, 1789–91
- CHARLOTTE SQUARE, Edinburgh, 1791–1807

Alberti, Leone Battista 1404–72
- FAÇADE, PALAZZO RUCELLAI, Florence 1446–51
- PALAZZO PITTI, Florence, 1458–66
- FAÇADE, SANTA MARIA NOVELLA, Florence 1460–67
- SANT'ANDREA, Mantua, begun 1470

Arup, Ove 1895–1988
- SMITHSON'S SCHOOL, Hunstanton, Norfolk, 1950–1
- COLLEGE BUILDINGS FOR CORPUS CHRIST COLLEGE, Cambridge, 1965–71
- SOMERVILLE COLLEGE, Oxford, 1965–75
- FESTIVAL HALL, Liverpool, 1982–4
- LLOYD'S OFFICES, Chatham, Kent, 1983.

Behrens, Peter 1868–1940
- AEG TURBINE FACTORY, Berlin, 1909
- AEG SMALL MOTOR FACTORY, Berlin, 1910
- GERMAN EMBASSY, St Petersburg, 1911
- I.G. FARBEN, Hoechst Dyeworks, Frankfurt, 1920–24
- AEG ADMINISTRATIVE BUILDING, Berlin, 1937.

Bernini, Giovanni Lorenzo 1598–1680
- BALDACCHINO, St Peter's, Rome, begun 1624
- CORNARO CHAPEL, S.Maria della Vittoria, Rome, 1645–52
- PIAZZA NAVONA, Rome, 1648–51
- SANT'ANDREA AL QUIRINALE, Rome, 1658–70
- PIAZZA, St. Peter's, Rome 1656
- PALAZZO ODESCALCHI, Rome, Italy begun 1664
- SCALA REGIA, Vatican, Italy, 1663–6.

Borromini, Francesco 1599–1667
- SAN CARLO ALLE QUATTRO FONTANE, Rome, 1634–43
- ORATORY OF ST PHILIP NERI, Rome, 1638–50
- SANT'IVO ALLA SAPIENZA, Rome, 1642–9
- COLLEGIO DI PROPAGANDA FIDE, Rome, Italy 1647–64
- SANT'AGNESE, Piazza Navona, Rome, 1653–7.

Bramante, Donato 1443/4–1514
- S.MARIA PRESSO S.SATIRO, Milan, Italy, begun 1482
- CLOISTER OF S.MARIA DELLA PACE, Rome, Italy, 1500
- TEMPIETTO OF S.PIETRO, Rome, Italy, after 1510
- SANTA CASA, Loreto 1509 onwards.

Breuer, Marcel 1902–81
- HARNISCHMACHER HOUSE, Wiesbaden, 1932
- BREUER HOUSE, Lincoln, Mass., 1939
- BREUER HOUSE, New Canaan, Conn., 1947 (*with Nervi and Zehrsuss*) UNESCO, Paris, 1951–8
- HUD BUILDING, Washington DC, 1967
- WHITNEY MUSEUM, New York, 1966.

Brunelleschi *see featured article.*

Burnham, Daniel, 1846–1912
- MONTAUK BUILDING, Chicago, 1881–2
- (*Burnham & Root*) ROOKERY BUILDING, Chicago, 1885–6
- (*Burnham & Root*) MONADNOCK BUILDING, Chicago, 1889–91
- (*D.H. Burnham& Co*) RELIANCE BUILDING, Chicago, 1890
- (*Burnham & Root*) ASHLAND BLOCK, Chicago 1891–2
- (*D.H. Burnham & Co*) FISHER BUILDING, Chicago
- (*D.H. Burnham & Co*) FLATIRON BUILDING, New York, 1902
- (*D.H. Burnham & Co*) RAILWAY EXCHANGE BUILDING, Chicago, 1903–4
- (*D.H. Burnham & Co*) UNION STATION, Washington DC, 1907.

Callicrates, 5th century BC
- PARTHENON, Athens, 447–438
- IONIC TEMPLE OF ATHENA AND NIKE ON ACROPOLIS, Athens, 448–421BC.

Campen, Jacob van 1595–1657
- COYMANS HOUSE, Amsterdam, 1624
- MAURITSHUIS, The Hague, 1633–5
- NOORDEINDE PALACE, The Hague, 1640
- TOWN HALL, Amsterdam, 1648–55
- NIEUWE KERK, Haarlem, 1645–
- ACCIJNHUIS THEATRE, Amsterdam, 1637.

Churriguera, Alberto (1676–1750); Joaquin (1674–1724); José Benitio (1665–1725)
- AYALA CHAPEL, Segovia Cathedral, 1686–7
- PLAZA MAYOR, Salamanca, begun 1728
- SAN ESTABAN, San Sebastian, begun 1711
- PARISH CHURCH, Orgaz, 1738
- FAÇADE, CHURCH OF THE ASSUMPTION, Rueda, 1738–47.

Corbusier *see featured article.*

Cuvilliés, Jean-François 1695–1768
- REICHE ZIMMER, Residenz, Munich, 1730–37
- AMALIENBURG, Schloss Nymphenburg, Munich, 1734–9
- RESIDENZTHEATER, Munich, 1751–3
- FAÇADE, THEATINERKIRCHE, Munich, 1767.

Delorme, Philibert c.1510–70
- CHÂTEAU D'ANET, Dreux, 1547–52
- BRIDGE AND GALLERY, Château de Chenonceaux, 1556–9.

Eiffel, Gustave 1832–1923
- EIFFEL TOWER, Paris, 1889
- DUORO BRIDGE, Portugal, 1876–7
- (*with Boileau*) BON MARCHÉ STORE, Paris, 1876
- ARMATURE, Statue of Liberty, New York, 1885.

Esherick, Joseph 1914–98
- GOLDMAN HOUSE, San Francisco, 1952
- CARY HOUSE, Mill Valley, California, 1960 (*with De Mars and Olsen*) Wurster Hall, Berkeley, 1964 (*with MLTW*) C-Ranch, Sonoma, 1965
- MONTEREY BAY AQUARIUM, California, 1984.

Fischer von Erlach, Johann Bernard 1656–1723
- DREIFALTIGKEITSKIRCHE, Salzburg, 1694–1702
- KOLLEGIENKIRCHE, Salzburg, 1694–1707
- TOWN PALACE OF PRINCE EUGEN OF SAVOY, Vienna, 1696–1700
- JOHANNESSPITALKIRCHE, Salzburg, 1699–1704
- KARLSKIRCHE, Vienna, begun 1715.

Floris, Cornelis 1514–75
- ANTWERP TOWN HALL, Antwerp, 1561–6
- HANSEATENHUIS, Antwerp, 1566
- ROOD SCREEN, Tournai Cathedral, 1572.

Fontaine, Pierre-François-Leonard 1762–1853
- ARC DU CAROUSEL, Paris, 1806–7
- RUE DE RIVOLI, Paris, 1801
- RESTORATION, PALAIS ROYAL, Paris, 1814–31
- HOTEL-DIEU, Pontoise, 1823–7.

Gaudí *see featured article.*

Gibbs, James 1682–1754
- ST MARY-LE-STRAND, London, 1714–24
- THE OCTAGON, Twickenham, 1720
- ST MARTIN'S IN THE FIELDS, London, 1722–6
- SENATE HOUSE, Cambridge, 1722–30
- DERBY CATHEDRAL, 1723–5
- KING'S COLLEGE FELLOWS' BUILDING, Cambridge University, 1724–49
- THE RADCLIFFE LIBRARY, Oxford University, 1737–49.

Gilbert, Cass 1859–1934
- WOOLWORTH BUILDING, New York, 1911
- NEW YORK LIFE ASSURANCE BUILDING, New York, 1925.

Gropius, Georg Walter Adolf 1883–1969
- FAGUS FACTORY, Alfeld-an-der-Leine, Germany, 1911
- ADMINISTRATIVE BUILDING, Werkbund Exhibition, Cologne, 1914
- BAUHAUS, Dessau, Germany, 1925–6
- SIEMENSSTADT HOUSING PROJECT, Germany, 1929
- IMPINGTON VILLAGE COLLEGE, Cambridge, UK, 1934–37
- GROPIUS HOUSE, Lincoln, Mass, 1937
- GRADUATE CENTER, Harvard University, Cambridge, Mass. 1949
- BAUHAUSARCHIV, Berlin, designed 1964, built 1976–78.

Guimard, Héctor 1867–1942
- CASTEL BÉRANGER, Paris, 1894–1912
- MÉTRO STATIONS, Paris, 1899–1913
- HÔTEL GUIMARD, Paris, 1912.

Hardouin-Mansart, Jules 1646–1708
- GRAND TRIANON AND CHAPEL, Versailles, begun 1678
- DOME OF THE INVALIDES CHAPEL, Paris, 1680–91
- PLACE VENDÔME, Paris, begun 1698.

Harrison, Peter 1716–76
- REDWOOD LIBRARY, Newport, Rhode Island, 1748–50
- KING'S CHAPEL, Boston, 1749–58
- TOURO SYNAGOGUE, Newport, Rhode Island, 1759
- CHRIST CHURCH, Cambridge, Mass., 1760–1
- BRICK MARKET, Newport, Rhode Island, 1761–72

Hawksmoor, Nicholas 1661–1736
- (*with Vanbrugh*) CASTLE HOWARD, 1699–1712
- (*with Vanbrugh*) BLENHEIM PALACE, 1705–24
- ST ALPHEGE, Greenwich, London, 1712–4
- CLARENDON BUILDING, Oxford, 1712–65
- ST ANNE'S, Limehouse, London, 1714–30
- CHRIST CHURCH, Spitalfields, London, 1714–29
- ST GEORGE-IN-THE-EAST, Stepney, London, 1714–29
- QUADRANGLE HALL & CODDINGTON LIBRARY, All Souls College, Oxford University, 1716–35
- West Tower, Westminster Abbey, London, 1718.

Herrera, Juan de 1530–97
- INFIRMARY AND CHAPEL, Toledo, 1574–82
- PALACE, Aranjuez, 1571–86
- EXCHANGE BUILDING, Seville, 1582
- VALLADOLID CATHEDRAL, c.1585.

Hildebrandt, Johann Lukas von 1668–1745
- SCHWARZENBERG PALACE, Vienna, 1697–1714
- BELVEDERE, Vienna, 1714–24
- PIARISTENKIRCHE, Vienna, 1714–46
- SEMINARKIRCHE, Linz, Austria, 1717–25
- PARISH CHURCH, Gollersdorf, Austria, 1740–1.

Hoban, James 1762–1831
- STATE CAPITOL, Columbia, completed 1791
- WHITE HOUSE, Washington DC, 1793–1801
- STATE AND WAR OFFICES, Washington DC, 1818.

Holobird & Roche, William Holobird 1854–1923; Martin Roche 1853–1927
- TACOMA BUILDING, Chicago, 1886–7
- MARQUETTE BUILDING, Chicago, 1893–4
- MCCLURG (*Crown*) BUILDING, Chicago, 1899.

Hood, Raymond Mathewson 1881–1934
- CHICAGO TRIBUNE BUILDING, 1923–5
- AMERICAN RADIATOR CO. BUILDING, New York, 1924
- DAILY NEWS BUILDING, New York, 1929
- ROCKEFELLER CENTER, New York, 1931–4
- RCA BUILDING, New York, 1934
- MCGRAW HILL BUILDING, New York, 1930–2.

Howe, George 1886–1955
- (*with Lescaze*) PSFS BUILDING, Philadelphia, 1929–32
- FORTUNE ROCK, Mount Deseret, Maine, 1938.

Hunt, Richard Morris 1827–95
- J.N.H GRISWOLD HOUSE, Newport, Rhode Island, 1862
- TRIBUNE BUILDING, New York, 1873
- 'BILTMORE', Ashville, N. Carolina, 1888–95
- 'THE BREAKERS', Newport, Rhode Island, 1892–45
- J.J ASTOR HOUSE, Newport, Rhode Island, 1893
- ENTRANCE WING, Metropolitan Museum of Art, New York, 1894–1902.

Imhotep, between 2780–2680BC
- STEP PYRAMID AT SAQQARA, Egypt, c.2778BC.

Jacobsen, Arne 1902–70
- BELLAVISTA HOUSING, Klampenborg near Copenhagen, 1934
- TOWN HALL, Aårhus, 1938–42
- MUNKEGAARDS SCHOOL, Gentofte, 1952–56
- TOWN HALL OF RODOVRE, Copenhagen, 1955–6
- SAS HOTEL, Copenhagen, 1960
- St CATHERINE'S COLLEGE, Oxford University, 1964.

Jefferson, Thomas, 1743–1826
- MONTICELLO, Virginia, 1768–82 and 1796–1809
- VIRGINIA STATE CAPITOL, Virginia, completed 1796
- UNIVERSITY OF VIRGINIA, Charlottesville, Virginia, 1817–26.

Jones, Inigo 1573–1652
- THE QUEEN'S HOUSE, Greenwich, 1616–35
- THE PRINCE'S LODGING, Newmarket, Suffolk, 1619–22
- BANQUETING HOUSE, Whitehall, London, 1619–22
- QUEEN'S CHAPEL, St James's Palace, London, 1623–7
- ST PAUL'S CHURCH, Covent Garden, London, 1631–3
- PIAZZA, Covent Garden, London, 1631–7.

Johnson, Philip Cortelyou b.1903
- JOHNSON HOUSE AND ADDITIONS, New Canaan, 1949 (*with Mies van der Rohe*)
- SEAGRAM BUILDING, New York,1956
- FOUR SEASONS RESTAURANT, New York, 1959
- AT&T BUILDING, New York, 1979–84.

Kahn, Louis 1901–74
- YALE ART GALLERY, New Haven, 1951
- RICHARDS MEDICAL LABORATORY, Philadelphia, 1957–64
- SALK INSTITUTE, La Jolla, California, 1959–63
- KIMBELL ART MUSEUM, Fort Worth, Texas, 1966–72
- CENTER FOR BRITISH ART & STUDIES, Yale, 1969–72.

Kent, William 1685–1748
- HOLKHAM HALL, Norfolk, 1734
- THE TREASURY, London, 1733–7
- 22 ARLINGTON ST, London, 1741
- 44 BERKELEY SQUARE, London, 1742–4
- HORSE GUARDS, London, 1750–9.

Key, Lieven de 1560–1627
- FAÇADE, LEIDEN TOWN HALL, 1594–7
- THE WEIGH HOUSE, Haarlem, 1598
- BUTCHERS GUILD HALL, Haarlem, 1602–3
- TOWER, NIEUWEKERK, Haarlem, 1613.

Labrouste, Henri 1801–75
- BIBLIOTHÈQUE STE GENEVIÈVE, Paris, designed 1838
- BIBLIOTHÈQUE NATIONAL, Paris, begun 1854.